TEACHER'S PET PUBLICATIONS

PUZZLE PACK
for
Hamlet

based on the play by
William Shakespeare

Written by
William T. Collins

© 2005 Teacher's Pet Publications
All Rights Reserved

The materials in this packet are copyrighted
by Teacher's Pet Publications, Inc.

These pages may be duplicated by the purchaser
for use in the purchaser's own classroom.

Copying any of these materials and distributing them
for any other purpose is a violation of the copyright laws.

© 2005 Teacher's Pet Publications, Inc.
www.tpet.com

INTRODUCTION

If you already own the LitPlan for this title, this Puzzle Pack will refresh your Unit Resource Materials and Vocabulary Resource Materials sections plus give you additional materials you can substitute into the tests. If you do not already have a complete LitPlan, these pages will give you some supplemental materials to use with your own plan. There are two main groups of materials: one set for unit words (such as characters' names, symbols, places, etc.) and one set for vocabulary words associated with the book.

WORD LIST

There is a word list for both the unit words and the vocabulary words. These lists show you which words are being used in the materials and the clues or definitions being used for those words. You may want to give students a word list with clues/definitions to help them, or you may want students to only have a word list (without clues/definitions) if you want them to work a little harder. Both are available for duplication. The word lists can also be your "calling key" for the bingo games.

FILL IN THE BLANK AND MATCHING

There are 4 each of the fill in the blank and matching worksheets for both the unit and vocabulary words. These pages can be used either as extra worksheets for students or as objective parts of a unit test. They can be done individually if students need extra help or as a whole class activity to review the material covered.

MAGIC SQUARES

The magic squares not only reinforce the material covered but also work on reasoning and math skills. Many teachers have told us that their students really enjoy doing these!

WORD SEARCH PUZZLES

The word search words go in all directions, as indicated on your answer keys. Two of the word search puzzles have the clues listed rather than the words. This makes the puzzle a little more difficult, but it reinforces the material better. Two word search puzzles have words only for students who find the clue puzzles too difficult.

CROSSWORD PUZZLES

Both unit and vocabulary word sections have 4 crossword puzzles.

BINGO CARDS

There are 32 individual bingo cards for the unit words and 32 individual bingo cards for the vocabulary words. You can use your word list as a "call list," calling the words at random and marking them off of your list as you go, or you could use the flash cards by cutting them apart and drawing the words at random from a hat (or box or whatever). To make a better review, you might ask for the definition and spelling of each word as you call it out–or you could call out the definitions and have students tell you the words they need to look for on the puzzle.

JUGGLE LETTERS

The vocabulary juggle letter game is intended to help students learn the spellings of the words. One sheet has the definitions listed on it as an extra help for students who need it or to reinforce the definitions if you choose to do so.

FLASH CARDS

We've included a set of vocabulary flash cards you can duplicate, cut, and fold for your students. Some teachers make a few sets for general use by the class; others make a set for each student. Some teachers duplicate them for each student and have the students cut & fold their own. You can cut out just the words and put them in a hat, have each student pick out one word and write the definition and a sentence for that word. Students then swap words and papers, with the next student adding a sentence of his own under the last one. You can have students swap as many times as you like. Each time the student will read the sentences written prior to his own and then add a sentence. You can cut out the words and definitions separately and play "I Have; Who Has?" Each student in the room draws a word and definition. The first student says, "I have (the name of the word). Who has the definition?" The student with the definition reads it then says, "I have (the name of the vocabulary word she has). Who has the definition?" The round continues until all words and definitions have been given.

Hamlet Word List

No.	Word	Clue/Definition
1.	BE	To ____ or not to ____
2.	BORROWER	Neither a ____ nor a lender be.
3.	CAT	The ____ will mew and the dog will have his day.
4.	CLAUDIUS	Hamlet's uncle, the new King
5.	CRUEL	I must be ____ only to be kind.
6.	DAGGERS	I will speak ____ to her, but use none.
7.	DEATH	Hamlet wonders whether a miserable life is better than the unknown of ____
8.	DENMARK	Something is rotten in the state of ____.
9.	DRINK	The queen dies after taking the poisoned ____ meant for Hamlet
10.	ELSINORE	Hamlet's home
11.	ENGLAND	Rosencrantz and Guildenstern prepare to take Hamlet there
12.	FORTINBRAS	Prince of Norway; wants to regain lands his father lost
13.	GERTRUDE	Hamlet's mother
14.	GHOST	Hamlet sees the ____ of his father
15.	GRAVE	Hamlet jumps into Ophelia's ____
16.	GUILDENSTERN	Rosencrantz and ____
17.	HAMLET	Sees his father's ghost and plans to get revenge for his father's murder
18.	HEAVEN	Leave her to ____/ And to those thorns that in her bosom lodge...
19.	HORATIO	Old schoolmate and friend of Hamlet
20.	KILLED	Claudius wants Hamlet ____ when he reaches England
21.	KIN	A little more than ____ & less than kind
22.	KING	The ____, the ____'s to blame.
23.	LAERTES	Polonius' son
24.	MAD	Polonius thinks Hamlet has gone ____ because of Ophelia's rejections
25.	METHOD	Though this be madness, yet there is ____ in't.
26.	OPHELIA	She goes crazy and drowns
27.	OSRIC	Tells Hamlet of the wager the King made on Hamlet's behalf
28.	PLAY	The ____'s the thing
29.	POISON	The ____ on Laertes sword kills Hamlet
30.	POLONIUS	Ophelia's father
31.	PROTEST	The lady doth ____ too much, methinks.
32.	REJECT	Polonius & Laertes tell Ophelia to ____ Hamlet's affections
33.	REVENGE	Laertes wants ____ for his father's death
34.	ROSENCRANTZ	____ & Guildenstern
35.	SEEMS	____, madam! Nay, it is. I know not ____.
36.	SOLILOQUY	Monologue by a character
37.	SPONGE	Descriptive word Hamlet uses for Rosencrantz and Guildenstern
38.	SWEETS	____ to the ____
39.	TAPESTRY	Hamlet runs his sword through it, killing Polonius who was hiding there
40.	THINKING	There is nothing either good or bad but ____ makes it so.
41.	TIME	The ____ is out of joint
42.	WOMAN	Frailty, thy name is ____!
43.	YORICK	Alas, poor ____! I knew him, Horatio.

Hamlet Fill In The Blank 1

_____
_____
_____
_____
_____
_____
_____
_____
_____
_____
_____
_____
_____
_____
_____
_____
_____
_____
_____
_____

1. Rosencrantz and ____
2. Hamlet's uncle, the new King
3. Prince of Norway; wants to regain lands his father lost
4. Hamlet sees the ____ of his father
5. Tells Hamlet of the wager the King made on Hamlet's behalf
6. The lady doth ____ too much, methinks.
7. Hamlet wonders whether a miserable life is better than the unknown of ____
8. Frailty, thy name is ____!
9. The ____ on Laertes sword kills Hamlet
10. ____ & Guildenstern
11. Rosencrantz and Guildenstern prepare to take Hamlet there
12. ____ to the ____
13. Claudius wants Hamlet ____ when he reaches England
14. Hamlet runs his sword through it, killing Polonius who was hiding there
15. Monologue by a character
16. Ophelia's father
17. To ____ or not to ____
18. She goes crazy and drowns
19. The queen dies after taking the poisoned ____ meant for Hamlet
20. Neither a ____ nor a lender be.

Hamlet Fill In The Blank 1 Answer Key

GUILDENSTERN	1. Rosencrantz and ____
CLAUDIUS	2. Hamlet's uncle, the new King
FORTINBRAS	3. Prince of Norway; wants to regain lands his father lost
GHOST	4. Hamlet sees the ____ of his father
OSRIC	5. Tells Hamlet of the wager the King made on Hamlet's behalf
PROTEST	6. The lady doth ____ too much, methinks.
DEATH	7. Hamlet wonders whether a miserable life is better than the unknown of ____
WOMAN	8. Frailty, thy name is ____ !
POISON	9. The ____ on Laertes sword kills Hamlet
ROSENCRANTZ	10. ____ & Guildenstern
ENGLAND	11. Rosencrantz and Guildenstern prepare to take Hamlet there
SWEETS	12. ____ to the ____
KILLED	13. Claudius wants Hamlet ____ when he reaches England
TAPESTRY	14. Hamlet runs his sword through it, killing Polonius who was hiding there
SOLILOQUY	15. Monologue by a character
POLONIUS	16. Ophelia's father
BE	17. To ____ or not to ____
OPHELIA	18. She goes crazy and drowns
DRINK	19. The queen dies after taking the poisoned ____ meant for Hamlet
BORROWER	20. Neither a ____ nor a lender be.

Hamlet Fill In The Blank 2

1. Frailty, thy name is ____!
2. Hamlet's mother
3. Hamlet runs his sword through it, killing Polonius who was hiding there
4. Polonius thinks Hamlet has gone ____ because of Ophelia's rejections
5. The ____ on Laertes sword kills Hamlet
6. The queen dies after taking the poisoned ____ meant for Hamlet
7. Rosencrantz and Guildenstern prepare to take Hamlet there
8. Hamlet's home
9. Sees his father's ghost and plans to get revenge for his father's murder
10. ____, madam! Nay, it is. I know not ____.
11. To ____ or not to ____
12. Ophelia's father
13. Laertes wants ____ for his father's death
14. A little more than ____ & less than kind
15. The ____, the ____'s to blame.
16. Hamlet wonders whether a miserable life is better than the unknown of ____
17. Polonius' son
18. Neither a ____ nor a lender be.
19. The ____'s the thing
20. The lady doth ____ too much, methinks.

Hamlet Fill In The Blank 2 Answer Key

WOMAN	1. Frailty, thy name is ____!
GERTRUDE	2. Hamlet's mother
TAPESTRY	3. Hamlet runs his sword through it, killing Polonius who was hiding there
MAD	4. Polonius thinks Hamlet has gone ____ because of Ophelia's rejections
POISON	5. The ____ on Laertes sword kills Hamlet
DRINK	6. The queen dies after taking the poisoned ____ meant for Hamlet
ENGLAND	7. Rosencrantz and Guildenstern prepare to take Hamlet there
ELSINORE	8. Hamlet's home
HAMLET	9. Sees his father's ghost and plans to get revenge for his father's murder
SEEMS	10. ____, madam! Nay, it is. I know not ____.
BE	11. To ____ or not to ____
POLONIUS	12. Ophelia's father
REVENGE	13. Laertes wants ____ for his father's death
KIN	14. A little more than ____ & less than kind
KING	15. The ____, the ____'s to blame.
DEATH	16. Hamlet wonders whether a miserable life is better than the unknown of ____
LAERTES	17. Polonius' son
BORROWER	18. Neither a ____ nor a lender be.
PLAY	19. The ____'s the thing
PROTEST	20. The lady doth ____ too much, methinks.

Hamlet Fill In The Blank 3

_____

_____

_____

_____

_____

_____

_____

_____

_____

_____

_____

_____

_____

_____

_____

_____

_____

_____

_____

_____

1. Hamlet's mother
2. Prince of Norway; wants to regain lands his father lost
3. Leave her to ____ / And to those thorns that in her bosom lodge...
4. Monologue by a character
5. I must be ____ only to be kind.
6. Tells Hamlet of the wager the King made on Hamlet's behalf
7. Polonius & Laertes tell Ophelia to ____ Hamlet's affections
8. Hamlet's home
9. Ophelia's father
10. The queen dies after taking the poisoned ____ meant for Hamlet
11. To ____ or not to ____
12. The ____, the ____'s to blame.
13. Though this be madness, yet there is ____ in't.
14. Hamlet jumps into Ophelia's ____
15. ____, madam! Nay, it is. I know not ____.
16. The ____ on Laertes sword kills Hamlet
17. Hamlet wonders whether a miserable life is better than the unknown of ____
18. There is nothing either good or bad but ____ makes it so.
19. Neither a ____ nor a lender be.
20. Descriptive word Hamlet uses for Rosencrantz and Guildenstern

Hamlet Fill In The Blank 3 Answer Key

GERTRUDE	1. Hamlet's mother
FORTINBRAS	2. Prince of Norway; wants to regain lands his father lost
HEAVEN	3. Leave her to ____/ And to those thorns that in her bosom lodge...
SOLILOQUY	4. Monologue by a character
CRUEL	5. I must be ____ only to be kind.
OSRIC	6. Tells Hamlet of the wager the King made on Hamlet's behalf
REJECT	7. Polonius & Laertes tell Ophelia to ____ Hamlet's affections
ELSINORE	8. Hamlet's home
POLONIUS	9. Ophelia's father
DRINK	10. The queen dies after taking the poisoned ____ meant for Hamlet
BE	11. To ____ or not to ____
KING	12. The ____, the ____'s to blame.
METHOD	13. Though this be madness, yet there is ____ in't.
GRAVE	14. Hamlet jumps into Ophelia's ____
SEEMS	15. ____, madam! Nay, it is. I know not ____.
POISON	16. The ____ on Laertes sword kills Hamlet
DEATH	17. Hamlet wonders whether a miserable life is better than the unknown of ____
THINKING	18. There is nothing either good or bad but ____ makes it so.
BORROWER	19. Neither a ____ nor a lender be.
SPONGE	20. Descriptive word Hamlet uses for Rosencrantz and Guildenstern

Hamlet Fill In The Blank 4

_____

_____

_____

_____

_____

_____

_____

_____

_____

_____

_____

_____

_____

_____

_____

_____

_____

_____

_____

_____

1. Tells Hamlet of the wager the King made on Hamlet's behalf
2. Hamlet's uncle, the new King
3. To _____ or not to _____
4. Hamlet wonders whether a miserable life is better than the unknown of _____
5. Alas, poor _____! I knew him, Horatio.
6. The _____ will mew and the dog will have his day.
7. Ophelia's father
8. I will speak _____ to her, but use none.
9. The _____ is out of joint
10. The _____ on Laertes sword kills Hamlet
11. Something is rotten in the state of _____.
12. Hamlet runs his sword through it, killing Polonius who was hiding there
13. Polonius & Laertes tell Ophelia to _____ Hamlet's affections
14. Descriptive word Hamlet uses for Rosencrantz and Guildenstern
15. Monologue by a character
16. _____, madam! Nay, it is. I know not _____.
17. Hamlet's home
18. Old schoolmate and friend of Hamlet
19. Leave her to _____/ And to those thorns that in her bosom lodge...
20. I must be _____ only to be kind.

Hamlet Fill In The Blank 4 Answer Key

OSRIC	1. Tells Hamlet of the wager the King made on Hamlet's behalf
CLAUDIUS	2. Hamlet's uncle, the new King
BE	3. To ____ or not to ____
DEATH	4. Hamlet wonders whether a miserable life is better than the unknown of ____
YORICK	5. Alas, poor ____! I knew him, Horatio.
CAT	6. The ____ will mew and the dog will have his day.
POLONIUS	7. Ophelia's father
DAGGERS	8. I will speak ____ to her, but use none.
TIME	9. The ____ is out of joint
POISON	10. The ____ on Laertes sword kills Hamlet
DENMARK	11. Something is rotten in the state of ____.
TAPESTRY	12. Hamlet runs his sword through it, killing Polonius who was hiding there
REJECT	13. Polonius & Laertes tell Ophelia to ____ Hamlet's affections
SPONGE	14. Descriptive word Hamlet uses for Rosencrantz and Guildenstern
SOLILOQUY	15. Monologue by a character
SEEMS	16. ____, madam! Nay, it is. I know not ____.
ELSINORE	17. Hamlet's home
HORATIO	18. Old schoolmate and friend of Hamlet
HEAVEN	19. Leave her to ____/ And to those thorns that in her bosom lodge...
CRUEL	20. I must be ____ only to be kind.

Hamlet Matching 1

___ 1. GUILDENSTERN   A. Polonius' son
___ 2. HEAVEN   B. ____ & Guildenstern
___ 3. OPHELIA   C. The lady doth ____ too much, methinks.
___ 4. SPONGE   D. Polonius thinks Hamlet has gone ____ because of Ophelia's rejections
___ 5. OSRIC   E. Rosencrantz and ____
___ 6. TIME   F. Hamlet's uncle, the new King
___ 7. CLAUDIUS   G. I will speak ____ to her, but use none.
___ 8. CAT   H. The ____ will mew and the dog will have his day.
___ 9. GERTRUDE   I. Hamlet's mother
___10. THINKING   J. She goes crazy and drowns
___11. LAERTES   K. Descriptive word Hamlet uses for Rosencrantz and Guildenstern
___12. KIN   L. Hamlet wonders whether a miserable life is better than the unknown of ____
___13. MAD   M. Leave her to ____/ And to those thorns that in her bosom lodge...
___14. METHOD   N. There is nothing either good or bad but ____ makes it so.
___15. ROSENCRANTZ   O. Hamlet jumps into Ophelia's ____
___16. KILLED   P. Neither a ____ nor a lender be.
___17. PROTEST   Q. A little more than ____ & less than kind
___18. DAGGERS   R. Claudius wants Hamlet ____ when he reaches England
___19. REJECT   S. The queen dies after taking the poisoned ____ meant for Hamlet
___20. BORROWER   T. Hamlet sees the ____ of his father
___21. GRAVE   U. Prince of Norway; wants to regain lands his father lost
___22. DEATH   V. Tells Hamlet of the wager the King made on Hamlet's behalf
___23. GHOST   W. Polonius & Laertes tell Ophelia to ____ Hamlet's affections
___24. FORTINBRAS   X. Though this be madness, yet there is ____ in't.
___25. DRINK   Y. The ____ is out of joint

Hamlet Matching 1 Answer Key

E - 1. GUILDENSTERN	A.	Polonius' son
M - 2. HEAVEN	B.	____ & Guildenstern
J - 3. OPHELIA	C.	The lady doth ____ too much, methinks.
K - 4. SPONGE	D.	Polonius thinks Hamlet has gone ____ because of Ophelia's rejections
V - 5. OSRIC	E.	Rosencrantz and ____
Y - 6. TIME	F.	Hamlet's uncle, the new King
F - 7. CLAUDIUS	G.	I will speak ____ to her, but use none.
H - 8. CAT	H.	The ____ will mew and the dog will have his day.
I - 9. GERTRUDE	I.	Hamlet's mother
N -10. THINKING	J.	She goes crazy and drowns
A -11. LAERTES	K.	Descriptive word Hamlet uses for Rosencrantz and Guildenstern
Q -12. KIN	L.	Hamlet wonders whether a miserable life is better than the unknown of ____
D -13. MAD	M.	Leave her to ____/ And to those thorns that in her bosom lodge...
X -14. METHOD	N.	There is nothing either good or bad but ____ makes it so.
B -15. ROSENCRANTZ	O.	Hamlet jumps into Ophelia's ____
R -16. KILLED	P.	Neither a ____ nor a lender be.
C -17. PROTEST	Q.	A little more than ____ & less than kind
G -18. DAGGERS	R.	Claudius wants Hamlet ____ when he reaches England
W -19. REJECT	S.	The queen dies after taking the poisoned ____ meant for Hamlet
P -20. BORROWER	T.	Hamlet sees the ____ of his father
O -21. GRAVE	U.	Prince of Norway; wants to regain lands his father lost
L -22. DEATH	V.	Tells Hamlet of the wager the King made on Hamlet's behalf
T -23. GHOST	W.	Polonius & Laertes tell Ophelia to ____ Hamlet's affections
U -24. FORTINBRAS	X.	Though this be madness, yet there is ____ in't.
S -25. DRINK	Y.	The ____ is out of joint

Hamlet Matching 2

___ 1. BE
___ 2. TIME
___ 3. POLONIUS
___ 4. WOMAN
___ 5. BORROWER
___ 6. PLAY
___ 7. CRUEL
___ 8. DEATH
___ 9. POISON
___ 10. LAERTES
___ 11. GHOST
___ 12. CLAUDIUS
___ 13. HEAVEN
___ 14. THINKING
___ 15. METHOD
___ 16. ELSINORE
___ 17. GUILDENSTERN
___ 18. OSRIC
___ 19. YORICK
___ 20. SEEMS
___ 21. DENMARK
___ 22. FORTINBRAS
___ 23. KILLED
___ 24. GERTRUDE
___ 25. REJECT

A. Neither a ____ nor a lender be.
B. Hamlet sees the ____ of his father
C. Rosencrantz and ____
D. Claudius wants Hamlet ____ when he reaches England
E. Though this be madness, yet there is ____ in't.
F. Something is rotten in the state of ____.
G. Hamlet wonders whether a miserable life is better than the unknown of ____
H. The ____ is out of joint
I. Tells Hamlet of the wager the King made on Hamlet's behalf
J. Alas, poor ____! I knew him, Horatio.
K. Polonius' son
L. There is nothing either good or bad but ____ makes it so.
M. Polonius & Laertes tell Ophelia to ____ Hamlet's affections
N. Leave her to ____/ And to those thorns that in her bosom lodge...
O. ____, madam! Nay, it is. I know not ____.
P. To ____ or not to ____
Q. I must be ____ only to be kind.
R. The ____ on Laertes sword kills Hamlet
S. Hamlet's mother
T. Hamlet's home
U. Frailty, thy name is ____!
V. Hamlet's uncle, the new King
W. The ____'s the thing
X. Prince of Norway; wants to regain lands his father lost
Y. Ophelia's father

Hamlet Matching 2 Answer Key

P - 1. BE	A. Neither a ____ nor a lender be.
H - 2. TIME	B. Hamlet sees the ____ of his father
Y - 3. POLONIUS	C. Rosencrantz and ____
U - 4. WOMAN	D. Claudius wants Hamlet ____ when he reaches England
A - 5. BORROWER	E. Though this be madness, yet there is ____ in't.
W - 6. PLAY	F. Something is rotten in the state of ____.
Q - 7. CRUEL	G. Hamlet wonders whether a miserable life is better than the unknown of ____
G - 8. DEATH	H. The ____ is out of joint
R - 9. POISON	I. Tells Hamlet of the wager the King made on Hamlet's behalf
K - 10. LAERTES	J. Alas, poor ____! I knew him, Horatio.
B - 11. GHOST	K. Polonius' son
V - 12. CLAUDIUS	L. There is nothing either good or bad but ____ makes it so.
N - 13. HEAVEN	M. Polonius & Laertes tell Ophelia to ____ Hamlet's affections
L - 14. THINKING	N. Leave her to ____/ And to those thorns that in her bosom lodge...
E - 15. METHOD	O. ____, madam! Nay, it is. I know not ____.
T - 16. ELSINORE	P. To ____ or not to ____
C - 17. GUILDENSTERN	Q. I must be ____ only to be kind.
I - 18. OSRIC	R. The ____ on Laertes sword kills Hamlet
J - 19. YORICK	S. Hamlet's mother
O - 20. SEEMS	T. Hamlet's home
F - 21. DENMARK	U. Frailty, thy name is ____!
X - 22. FORTINBRAS	V. Hamlet's uncle, the new King
D - 23. KILLED	W. The ____'s the thing
S - 24. GERTRUDE	X. Prince of Norway; wants to regain lands his father lost
M - 25. REJECT	Y. Ophelia's father

Hamlet Matching 3

___ 1. TAPESTRY
___ 2. CLAUDIUS
___ 3. ELSINORE
___ 4. BORROWER
___ 5. GHOST
___ 6. DEATH
___ 7. CRUEL
___ 8. DAGGERS
___ 9. OPHELIA
___10. POLONIUS
___11. SPONGE
___12. ROSENCRANTZ
___13. SEEMS
___14. CAT
___15. REJECT
___16. OSRIC
___17. HAMLET
___18. HORATIO
___19. THINKING
___20. SOLILOQUY
___21. DRINK
___22. POISON
___23. PLAY
___24. REVENGE
___25. FORTINBRAS

A. Polonius & Laertes tell Ophelia to ____ Hamlet's affections
B. Descriptive word Hamlet uses for Rosencrantz and Guildenstern
C. Monologue by a character
D. Tells Hamlet of the wager the King made on Hamlet's behalf
E. Hamlet sees the ____ of his father
F. There is nothing either good or bad but ____ makes it so.
G. She goes crazy and drowns
H. Hamlet's uncle, the new King
I. The ____ on Laertes sword kills Hamlet
J. ____ & Guildenstern
K. Old schoolmate and friend of Hamlet
L. Hamlet runs his sword through it, killing Polonius who was hiding there
M. Hamlet wonders whether a miserable life is better than the unknown of ____
N. Neither a ____ nor a lender be.
O. Sees his father's ghost and plans to get revenge for his father's murder
P. The ____'s the thing
Q. I will speak ____ to her, but use none.
R. ____, madam! Nay, it is. I know not ____.
S. I must be ____ only to be kind.
T. The queen dies after taking the poisoned ____ meant for Hamlet
U. Laertes wants ____ for his father's death
V. The ____ will mew and the dog will have his day.
W. Hamlet's home
X. Ophelia's father
Y. Prince of Norway; wants to regain lands his father lost

Hamlet Matching 3 Answer Key

L - 1.	TAPESTRY	A.	Polonius & Laertes tell Ophelia to ____ Hamlet's affections
H - 2.	CLAUDIUS	B.	Descriptive word Hamlet uses for Rosencrantz and Guildenstern
W - 3.	ELSINORE	C.	Monologue by a character
N - 4.	BORROWER	D.	Tells Hamlet of the wager the King made on Hamlet's behalf
E - 5.	GHOST	E.	Hamlet sees the ____ of his father
M - 6.	DEATH	F.	There is nothing either good or bad but ____ makes it so.
S - 7.	CRUEL	G.	She goes crazy and drowns
Q - 8.	DAGGERS	H.	Hamlet's uncle, the new King
G - 9.	OPHELIA	I.	The ____ on Laertes sword kills Hamlet
X - 10.	POLONIUS	J.	____ & Guildenstern
B - 11.	SPONGE	K.	Old schoolmate and friend of Hamlet
J - 12.	ROSENCRANTZ	L.	Hamlet runs his sword through it, killing Polonius who was hiding there
R - 13.	SEEMS	M.	Hamlet wonders whether a miserable life is better than the unknown of ____
V - 14.	CAT	N.	Neither a ____ nor a lender be.
A - 15.	REJECT	O.	Sees his father's ghost and plans to get revenge for his father's murder
D - 16.	OSRIC	P.	The ____'s the thing
O - 17.	HAMLET	Q.	I will speak ____ to her, but use none.
K - 18.	HORATIO	R.	____, madam! Nay, it is. I know not ____.
F - 19.	THINKING	S.	I must be ____ only to be kind.
C - 20.	SOLILOQUY	T.	The queen dies after taking the poisoned ____ meant for Hamlet
T - 21.	DRINK	U.	Laertes wants ____ for his father's death
I - 22.	POISON	V.	The ____ will mew and the dog will have his day.
P - 23.	PLAY	W.	Hamlet's home
U - 24.	REVENGE	X.	Ophelia's father
Y - 25.	FORTINBRAS	Y.	Prince of Norway; wants to regain lands his father lost

Hamlet Matching 4

___ 1. HORATIO
___ 2. ELSINORE
___ 3. GERTRUDE
___ 4. CLAUDIUS
___ 5. PROTEST
___ 6. BORROWER
___ 7. ROSENCRANTZ
___ 8. METHOD
___ 9. ENGLAND
___ 10. DENMARK
___ 11. FORTINBRAS
___ 12. HAMLET
___ 13. CAT
___ 14. HEAVEN
___ 15. GRAVE
___ 16. KING
___ 17. KILLED
___ 18. THINKING
___ 19. OPHELIA
___ 20. DAGGERS
___ 21. GUILDENSTERN
___ 22. SWEETS
___ 23. LAERTES
___ 24. YORICK
___ 25. REJECT

A. She goes crazy and drowns
B. The lady doth ____ too much, methinks.
C. Rosencrantz and Guildenstern prepare to take Hamlet there
D. Something is rotten in the state of ____.
E. I will speak ____ to her, but use none.
F. Hamlet's home
G. Hamlet's mother
H. The ____ will mew and the dog will have his day.
I. Alas, poor ____! I knew him, Horatio.
J. The ____, the ____'s to blame.
K. Leave her to ____ / And to those thorns that in her bosom lodge...
L. ____ & Guildenstern
M. Hamlet's uncle, the new King
N. Neither a ____ nor a lender be.
O. Hamlet jumps into Ophelia's ____
P. Though this be madness, yet there is ____ in't.
Q. ____ to the ____
R. Polonius' son
S. There is nothing either good or bad but ____ makes it so.
T. Prince of Norway; wants to regain lands his father lost
U. Polonius & Laertes tell Ophelia to ____ Hamlet's affections
V. Rosencrantz and ____
W. Sees his father's ghost and plans to get revenge for his father's murder
X. Old schoolmate and friend of Hamlet
Y. Claudius wants Hamlet ____ when he reaches England

Hamlet Matching 4 Answer Key

X - 1. HORATIO	A. She goes crazy and drowns
F - 2. ELSINORE	B. The lady doth ____ too much, methinks.
G - 3. GERTRUDE	C. Rosencrantz and Guildenstern prepare to take Hamlet there
M - 4. CLAUDIUS	D. Something is rotten in the state of ____.
B - 5. PROTEST	E. I will speak ____ to her, but use none.
N - 6. BORROWER	F. Hamlet's home
L - 7. ROSENCRANTZ	G. Hamlet's mother
P - 8. METHOD	H. The ____ will mew and the dog will have his day.
C - 9. ENGLAND	I. Alas, poor ____! I knew him, Horatio.
D -10. DENMARK	J. The ____, the ____'s to blame.
T -11. FORTINBRAS	K. Leave her to ____/ And to those thorns that in her bosom lodge...
W -12. HAMLET	L. ____ & Guildenstern
H -13. CAT	M. Hamlet's uncle, the new King
K -14. HEAVEN	N. Neither a ____ nor a lender be.
O -15. GRAVE	O. Hamlet jumps into Ophelia's ____
J -16. KING	P. Though this be madness, yet there is ____ in't.
Y -17. KILLED	Q. ____ to the ____
S -18. THINKING	R. Polonius' son
A -19. OPHELIA	S. There is nothing either good or bad but ____ makes it so.
E -20. DAGGERS	T. Prince of Norway; wants to regain lands his father lost
V -21. GUILDENSTERN	U. Polonius & Laertes tell Ophelia to ____ Hamlet's affections
Q -22. SWEETS	V. Rosencrantz and ____
R -23. LAERTES	W. Sees his father's ghost and plans to get revenge for his father's murder
I - 24. YORICK	X. Old schoolmate and friend of Hamlet
U -25. REJECT	Y. Claudius wants Hamlet ____ when he reaches England

Hamlet Magic Squares 1

Match the definition with the vocabulary word. Put your answers in the magic squares below. When your answers are correct, all columns and rows will add to the same number.

A. DAGGERS
B. DRINK
C. WOMAN
D. GUILDENSTERN
E. HAMLET
F. DENMARK
G. PROTEST
H. OSRIC
I. FORTINBRAS
J. KING
K. TIME
L. HEAVEN
M. OPHELIA
N. TAPESTRY
O. METHOD
P. ENGLAND

1. Tells Hamlet of the wager the King made on Hamlet's behalf
2. I will speak ____ to her, but use none.
3. The queen dies after taking the poisoned ____ meant for Hamlet
4. The lady doth ____ too much, methinks.
5. The ____, the ____'s to blame.
6. Though this be madness, yet there is ____ in't.
7. Rosencrantz and Guildenstern prepare to take Hamlet there
8. Prince of Norway; wants to regain lands his father lost
9. The ____ is out of joint
10. Hamlet runs his sword through it, killing Polonius who was hiding there
11. She goes crazy and drowns
12. Leave her to ____/ And to those thorns that in her bosom lodge...
13. Sees his father's ghost and plans to get revenge for his father's murder
14. Rosencrantz and ____
15. Frailty, thy name is ____!
16. Something is rotten in the state of ____.

A=	B=	C=	D=
E=	F=	G=	H=
I=	J=	K=	L=
M=	N=	O=	P=

Hamlet Magic Squares 1 Answer Key

Match the definition with the vocabulary word. Put your answers in the magic squares below. When your answers are correct, all columns and rows will add to the same number.

A. DAGGERS
B. DRINK
C. WOMAN
D. GUILDENSTERN
E. HAMLET
F. DENMARK
G. PROTEST
H. OSRIC
I. FORTINBRAS
J. KING
K. TIME
L. HEAVEN
M. OPHELIA
N. TAPESTRY
O. METHOD
P. ENGLAND

1. Tells Hamlet of the wager the King made on Hamlet's behalf
2. I will speak ____ to her, but use none.
3. The queen dies after taking the poisoned ____ meant for Hamlet
4. The lady doth ____ too much, methinks.
5. The ____, the ____'s to blame.
6. Though this be madness, yet there is ____ in't.
7. Rosencrantz and Guildenstern prepare to take Hamlet there
8. Prince of Norway; wants to regain lands his father lost
9. The ____ is out of joint
10. Hamlet runs his sword through it, killing Polonius who was hiding there
11. She goes crazy and drowns
12. Leave her to ____/ And to those thorns that in her bosom lodge...
13. Sees his father's ghost and plans to get revenge for his father's murder
14. Rosencrantz and ____
15. Frailty, thy name is ____!
16. Something is rotten in the state of ____.

A=2	B=3	C=15	D=14
E=13	F=16	G=4	H=1
I=8	J=5	K=9	L=12
M=11	N=10	O=6	P=7

Hamlet Magic Squares 2

Match the definition with the vocabulary word. Put your answers in the magic squares below. When your answers are correct, all columns and rows will add to the same number.

A. POLONIUS
B. REVENGE
C. MAD
D. ROSENCRANTZ
E. OSRIC
F. TAPESTRY
G. GRAVE
H. KIN
I. PROTEST
J. WOMAN
K. KING
L. KILLED
M. ENGLAND
N. GHOST
O. GERTRUDE
P. DENMARK

1. Ophelia's father
2. Hamlet sees the ____ of his father
3. Frailty, thy name is ____!
4. Tells Hamlet of the wager the King made on Hamlet's behalf
5. Hamlet jumps into Ophelia's ____
6. Claudius wants Hamlet ____ when he reaches England
7. Something is rotten in the state of ____.
8. Polonius thinks Hamlet has gone ____ because of Ophelia's rejections
9. Hamlet's mother
10. ____ & Guildenstern
11. A little more than ____ & less than kind
12. The ____, the ____'s to blame.
13. The lady doth ____ too much, methinks.
14. Hamlet runs his sword through it, killing Polonius who was hiding there
15. Laertes wants ____ for his father's death
16. Rosencrantz and Guildenstern prepare to take Hamlet there

A=	B=	C=	D=
E=	F=	G=	H=
I=	J=	K=	L=
M=	N=	O=	P=

Hamlet Magic Squares 2 Answer Key

Match the definition with the vocabulary word. Put your answers in the magic squares below. When your answers are correct, all columns and rows will add to the same number.

A. POLONIUS
B. REVENGE
C. MAD
D. ROSENCRANTZ
E. OSRIC
F. TAPESTRY
G. GRAVE
H. KIN
I. PROTEST
J. WOMAN
K. KING
L. KILLED
M. ENGLAND
N. GHOST
O. GERTRUDE
P. DENMARK

1. Ophelia's father
2. Hamlet sees the ____ of his father
3. Frailty, thy name is ____!
4. Tells Hamlet of the wager the King made on Hamlet's behalf
5. Hamlet jumps into Ophelia's ____
6. Claudius wants Hamlet ____ when he reaches England
7. Something is rotten in the state of ____.
8. Polonius thinks Hamlet has gone ____ because of Ophelia's rejections
9. Hamlet's mother
10. ____ & Guildenstern
11. A little more than ____ & less than kind
12. The ____, the ____'s to blame.
13. The lady doth ____ too much, methinks.
14. Hamlet runs his sword through it, killing Polonius who was hiding there
15. Laertes wants ____ for his father's death
16. Rosencrantz and Guildenstern prepare to take Hamlet there

A=1	B=15	C=8	D=10
E=4	F=14	G=5	H=11
I=13	J=3	K=12	L=6
M=16	N=2	O=9	P=7

Hamlet Magic Squares 3

Match the definition with the vocabulary word. Put your answers in the magic squares below. When your answers are correct, all columns and rows will add to the same number.

A. PROTEST
B. KILLED
C. PLAY
D. BORROWER
E. CLAUDIUS
F. REJECT
G. KING
H. ENGLAND
I. HEAVEN
J. SPONGE
K. HAMLET
L. SWEETS
M. SEEMS
N. OPHELIA
O. TIME
P. MAD

1. The ____ is out of joint
2. Neither a ____ nor a lender be.
3. Descriptive word Hamlet uses for Rosencrantz and Guildenstern
4. Hamlet's uncle, the new King
5. Leave her to ____/ And to those thorns that in her bosom lodge...
6. Polonius & Laertes tell Ophelia to ____ Hamlet's affections
7. Polonius thinks Hamlet has gone ____ because of Ophelia's rejections
8. The ____'s the thing
9. Rosencrantz and Guildenstern prepare to take Hamlet there
10. Sees his father's ghost and plans to get revenge for his father's murder
11. The lady doth ____ too much, methinks.
12. She goes crazy and drowns
13. Claudius wants Hamlet ____ when he reaches England
14. ____, madam! Nay, it is. I know not ____.
15. The ____, the ____'s to blame.
16. ____ to the ____

A=	B=	C=	D=
E=	F=	G=	H=
I=	J=	K=	L=
M=	N=	O=	P=

Hamlet Magic Squares 3 Answer Key

Match the definition with the vocabulary word. Put your answers in the magic squares below. When your answers are correct, all columns and rows will add to the same number.

A. PROTEST
B. KILLED
C. PLAY
D. BORROWER
E. CLAUDIUS
F. REJECT
G. KING
H. ENGLAND
I. HEAVEN
J. SPONGE
K. HAMLET
L. SWEETS
M. SEEMS
N. OPHELIA
O. TIME
P. MAD

1. The ____ is out of joint
2. Neither a ____ nor a lender be.
3. Descriptive word Hamlet uses for Rosencrantz and Guildenstern
4. Hamlet's uncle, the new King
5. Leave her to ____/ And to those thorns that in her bosom lodge...
6. Polonius & Laertes tell Ophelia to ____ Hamlet's affections
7. Polonius thinks Hamlet has gone ____ because of Ophelia's rejections
8. The ____'s the thing
9. Rosencrantz and Guildenstern prepare to take Hamlet there
10. Sees his father's ghost and plans to get revenge for his father's murder
11. The lady doth ____ too much, methinks.
12. She goes crazy and drowns
13. Claudius wants Hamlet ____ when he reaches England
14. ____, madam! Nay, it is. I know not ____.
15. The ____, the ____'s to blame.
16. ____ to the ____

A=11	B=13	C=8	D=2
E=4	F=6	G=15	H=9
I=5	J=3	K=10	L=16
M=14	N=12	O=1	P=7

Hamlet Magic Squares 4

Match the definition with the vocabulary word. Put your answers in the magic squares below. When your answers are correct, all columns and rows will add to the same number.

A. SWEETS
B. HEAVEN
C. DENMARK
D. METHOD
E. POLONIUS
F. BORROWER
G. HAMLET
H. DEATH
I. TAPESTRY
J. HORATIO
K. OSRIC
L. REVENGE
M. GUILDENSTERN
N. WOMAN
O. KING
P. ELSINORE

1. Neither a ____ nor a lender be.
2. Hamlet runs his sword through it, killing Polonius who was hiding there
3. The ____, the ____'s to blame.
4. Though this be madness, yet there is ____ in't.
5. Rosencrantz and ____
6. Leave her to ____/ And to those thorns that in her bosom lodge...
7. Hamlet wonders whether a miserable life is better than the unknown of ____
8. Tells Hamlet of the wager the King made on Hamlet's behalf
9. Something is rotten in the state of ____.
10. Hamlet's home
11. Old schoolmate and friend of Hamlet
12. Ophelia's father
13. Laertes wants ____ for his father's death
14. Sees his father's ghost and plans to get revenge for his father's murder
15. ____ to the ____
16. Frailty, thy name is ____!

A=	B=	C=	D=
E=	F=	G=	H=
I=	J=	K=	L=
M=	N=	O=	P=

Hamlet Magic Squares 4 Answer Key

Match the definition with the vocabulary word. Put your answers in the magic squares below. When your answers are correct, all columns and rows will add to the same number.

A. SWEETS
B. HEAVEN
C. DENMARK
D. METHOD
E. POLONIUS
F. BORROWER
G. HAMLET
H. DEATH
I. TAPESTRY
J. HORATIO
K. OSRIC
L. REVENGE
M. GUILDENSTERN
N. WOMAN
O. KING
P. ELSINORE

1. Neither a ____ nor a lender be.
2. Hamlet runs his sword through it, killing Polonius who was hiding there
3. The ____, the ____'s to blame.
4. Though this be madness, yet there is ____ in't.
5. Rosencrantz and ____
6. Leave her to ____/ And to those thorns that in her bosom lodge...
7. Hamlet wonders whether a miserable life is better than the unknown of ____
8. Tells Hamlet of the wager the King made on Hamlet's behalf
9. Something is rotten in the state of ____.
10. Hamlet's home
11. Old schoolmate and friend of Hamlet
12. Ophelia's father
13. Laertes wants ____ for his father's death
14. Sees his father's ghost and plans to get revenge for his father's murder
15. ____ to the ____
16. Frailty, thy name is ____!

A=15	B=6	C=9	D=4
E=12	F=1	G=14	H=7
I=2	J=11	K=8	L=13
M=5	N=16	O=3	P=10

Hamlet Word Search 1

Words are placed backwards, forward, diagonally, up and down. Clues listed below can help you find the words. Circle the hidden vocabulary words in the maze.

```
G D A G G E R S B O R R O W E R T Y R C
R S R N M H Z Z M I O R P W P F I O E S
A O E I E Q O Y Y T S Z H Q R O M R J C
V L V K T C C S Y A E V E G O R E I E F
E I E N H J R D T R N P L U T T K C C X
Z L N I O D E U T O C D I I E I V K T N
K O G H D L B G E H R G A L S N K J Z K
W Q E T L F B K P L A T C D T B V W F L
W U L I P O I S O N N Q S E E R G L Z S
X Y K M J N T Y X D T Z B N S A S C C H
L S N Q C K T Z N C Z Y G S T S W Z C R
T A M K N L N V Q T R L R T H J E Q J J
A G E H C S A T M S A W T E T J E L V T
P V Z R A H V U A N B O N R J L T B Z H
E D U R T R E G D N D N S N M L S E R B
S J B A S E D P S I X R E Q L Y Z K T
T N E T P L S E H P U W E R I A G N I R
R D H E A V E N N Y O S M F L C I L N N
Y P O L O N I U S M L N S P Y R T I G J
P W J M D Y Z Z A D A D G Y D V K F J G
S X W A V Z G N B T P R W E M D L X N X
W B R H E L S I N O R E K K Y W W Z F J
```

A little more than ____ & less than kind (3)
Alas, poor ____! I knew him, Horatio. (6)
Claudius wants Hamlet ____ when he reaches England (6)
Descriptive word Hamlet uses for Rosencrantz and Guildenstern (6)
Frailty, thy name is ____! (5)
Hamlet jumps into Ophelia's ____ (5)
Hamlet runs his sword through it, killing Polonius who was hiding there (8)
Hamlet sees the ____ of his father (5)
Hamlet wonders whether a miserable life is better than the unknown of ____ (5)
Hamlet's home (8)
Hamlet's mother (8)
Hamlet's uncle, the new King (8)
I must be ____ only to be kind. (5)
I will speak ____ to her, but use none. (7)
Laertes wants ____ for his father's death (7)
Leave her to ____/ And to those thorns that in her bosom lodge... (6)
Monologue by a character (9)
Neither a ____ nor a lender be. (8)
Old schoolmate and friend of Hamlet (7)
Ophelia's father (8)
Polonius & Laertes tell Ophelia to ____ Hamlet's affections (6)
Polonius thinks Hamlet has gone ____ because of

Ophelia's rejections (3)
Polonius' son (7)
Prince of Norway; wants to regain lands his father lost (10)
Rosencrantz and Guildenstern prepare to take Hamlet there (7)
Rosencrantz and ____ (12)
Sees his father's ghost and plans to get revenge for his father's murder (6)
She goes crazy and drowns (7)
Something is rotten in the state of ____. (7)
Tells Hamlet of the wager the King made on Hamlet's behalf (5)
The ____ is out of joint (4)
The ____ on Laertes sword kills Hamlet (6)
The ____ will mew and the dog will have his day. (3)
The ____'s the thing (4)
The ____, the ____'s to blame. (4)
The lady doth ____ too much, methinks. (7)
The queen dies after taking the poisoned ____ meant for Hamlet (5)
There is nothing either good or bad but ____ makes it so. (8)
Though this be madness, yet there is ____ in't. (6)
To ____ or not to ____ (2)
____ & Guildenstern (11)
____ to the ____ (6)
____, madam! Nay, it is. I know not ____. (5)

Hamlet Word Search 1 Answer Key

Words are placed backwards, forward, diagonally, up and down. Clues listed below can help you find the words. Circle the hidden vocabulary words in the maze.

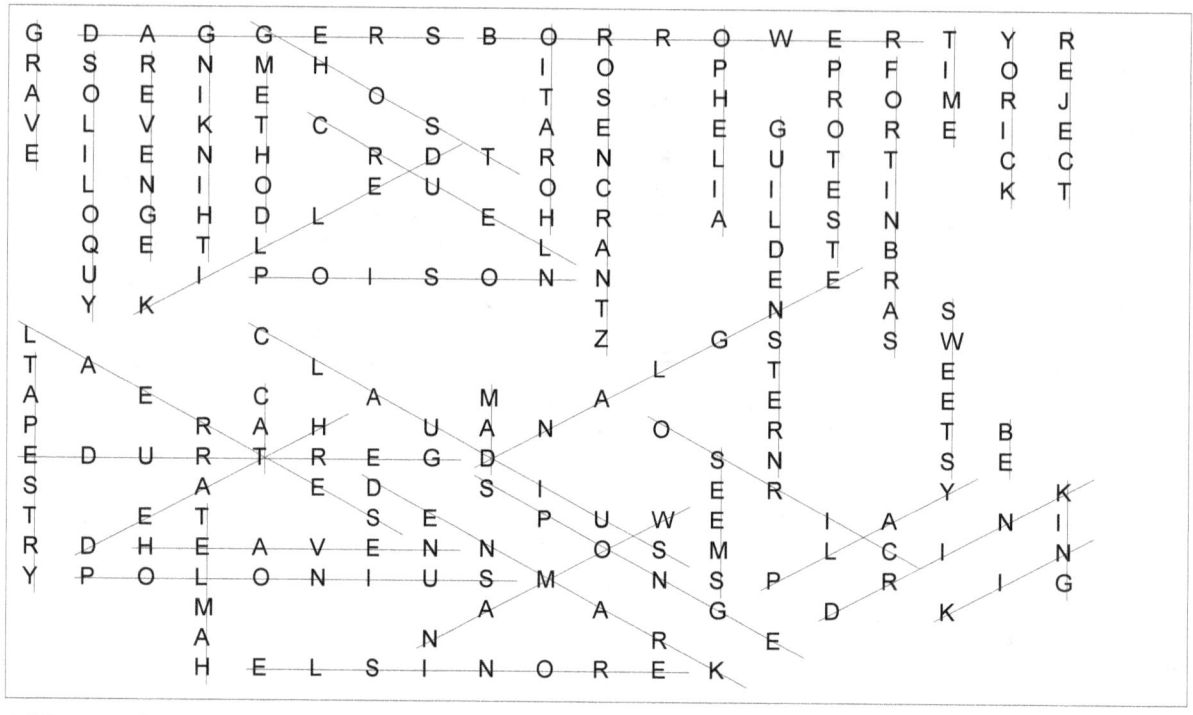

A little more than ____ & less than kind (3)
Alas, poor ____! I knew him, Horatio. (6)
Claudius wants Hamlet ____ when he reaches England (6)
Descriptive word Hamlet uses for Rosencrantz and Guildenstern (6)
Frailty, thy name is ____! (5)
Hamlet jumps into Ophelia's ____ (5)
Hamlet runs his sword through it, killing Polonius who was hiding there (8)
Hamlet sees the ____ of his father (5)
Hamlet wonders whether a miserable life is better than the unknown of ____ (5)
Hamlet's home (8)
Hamlet's mother (8)
Hamlet's uncle, the new King (8)
I must be ____ only to be kind. (5)
I will speak ____ to her, but use none. (7)
Laertes wants ____ for his father's death (7)
Leave her to ____/ And to those thorns that in her bosom lodge... (6)
Monologue by a character (9)
Neither a ____ nor a lender be. (8)
Old schoolmate and friend of Hamlet (7)
Ophelia's father (8)
Polonius & Laertes tell Ophelia to ____ Hamlet's affections (6)
Polonius thinks Hamlet has gone ____ because of

Ophelia's rejections (3)
Polonius' son (7)
Prince of Norway; wants to regain lands his father lost (10)
Rosencrantz and Guildenstern prepare to take Hamlet there (7)
Rosencrantz and ____ (12)
Sees his father's ghost and plans to get revenge for his father's murder (6)
She goes crazy and drowns (7)
Something is rotten in the state of ____. (7)
Tells Hamlet of the wager the King made on Hamlet's behalf (5)
The ____ is out of joint (4)
The ____ on Laertes sword kills Hamlet (6)
The ____ will mew and the dog will have his day. (3)
The ____'s the thing (4)
The ____, the ____'s to blame. (4)
The lady doth ____ too much, methinks. (7)
The queen dies after taking the poisoned ____ meant for Hamlet (5)
There is nothing either good or bad but ____ makes it so. (8)
Though this be madness, yet there is ____ in't. (6)
To ____ or not to ____ (2)
____ & Guildenstern (11)
____ to the ____ (6)
____, madam! Nay, it is. I know not ____. (5)

Hamlet Word Search 2

Words are placed backwards, forward, diagonally, up and down. Clues listed below can help you find the words. Circle the hidden vocabulary words in the maze.

```
G E R T R U D E S Z C P T B V K G P F L
H R J T X C R D O E G Y F H C W K O W B
K Y A W W L R A L G E F X I I Z L L J F
Z D S V G A O G I T Y M R B L N N O J X
J N J K E U S G L Y N O S B A B K N B K
R Z D I W D E E O Z Y M N G E O L I Q M
W X B L L I N R Q M Y W R R R R R U N P
R H M L L U C S U B R X E M T R L S X G
R T F E F S R R Y F T D T E E O Z V Z P
W B J D H W A R K Y S N S G S W R N Q P
T R H Z K I N R X N E K N N C E C P M J
C S B V L B T J T M P S E O K R A E D L
I G L E R X Z D H T A E D P R O T E S T
R P H G N K K R W R T N L S T H N I Z F
S P S G Q S I I B H A G I W O M Z S M T
O I T A R O H N L L B H U D A N N B E E
L M X C Y E I K G S K O G R A O E J J G
G B B Y R T J N T Q H S K M S J V F Q B
C M C Y R U E E K Y M T O I G G A K G Z
V B A O Z Z E J C I J W O R E V E N G E
X L F D B W M L R T N P J H H M H J D P
P D E L S I N O R E H A M L E T K M Y H
```

A little more than ____ & less than kind (3)
Alas, poor ____! I knew him, Horatio. (6)
Claudius wants Hamlet ____ when he reaches England (6)
Descriptive word Hamlet uses for Rosencrantz and Guildenstern (6)
Frailty, thy name is ____! (5)
Hamlet jumps into Ophelia's ____ (5)
Hamlet runs his sword through it, killing Polonius who was hiding there (8)
Hamlet sees the ____ of his father (5)
Hamlet wonders whether a miserable life is better than the unknown of ____ (5)
Hamlet's home (8)
Hamlet's mother (8)
Hamlet's uncle, the new King (8)
I must be ____ only to be kind. (5)
I will speak ____ to her, but use none. (7)
Laertes wants ____ for his father's death (7)
Leave her to ____/ And to those thorns that in her bosom lodge... (6)
Monologue by a character (9)
Neither a ____ nor a lender be. (8)
Old schoolmate and friend of Hamlet (7)
Ophelia's father (8)
Polonius & Laertes tell Ophelia to ____ Hamlet's affections (6)
Polonius thinks Hamlet has gone ____ because of

Ophelia's rejections (3)
Polonius' son (7)
Prince of Norway; wants to regain lands his father lost (10)
Rosencrantz and Guildenstern prepare to take Hamlet there (7)
Rosencrantz and ____ (12)
Sees his father's ghost and plans to get revenge for his father's murder (6)
She goes crazy and drowns (7)
Something is rotten in the state of ____. (7)
Tells Hamlet of the wager the King made on Hamlet's behalf (5)
The ____ is out of joint (4)
The ____ on Laertes sword kills Hamlet (6)
The ____ will mew and the dog will have his day. (3)
The ____'s the thing (4)
The ____, the ____'s to blame. (4)
The lady doth ____ too much, methinks. (7)
The queen dies after taking the poisoned ____ meant for Hamlet (5)
There is nothing either good or bad but ____ makes it so. (8)
Though this be madness, yet there is ____ in't. (6)
To ____ or not to ____ (2)
____ & Guildenstern (11)
____ to the ____ (6)
____, madam! Nay, it is. I know not ____. (5)

Hamlet Word Search 2 Answer Key

Words are placed backwards, forward, diagonally, up and down. Clues listed below can help you find the words. Circle the hidden vocabulary words in the maze.

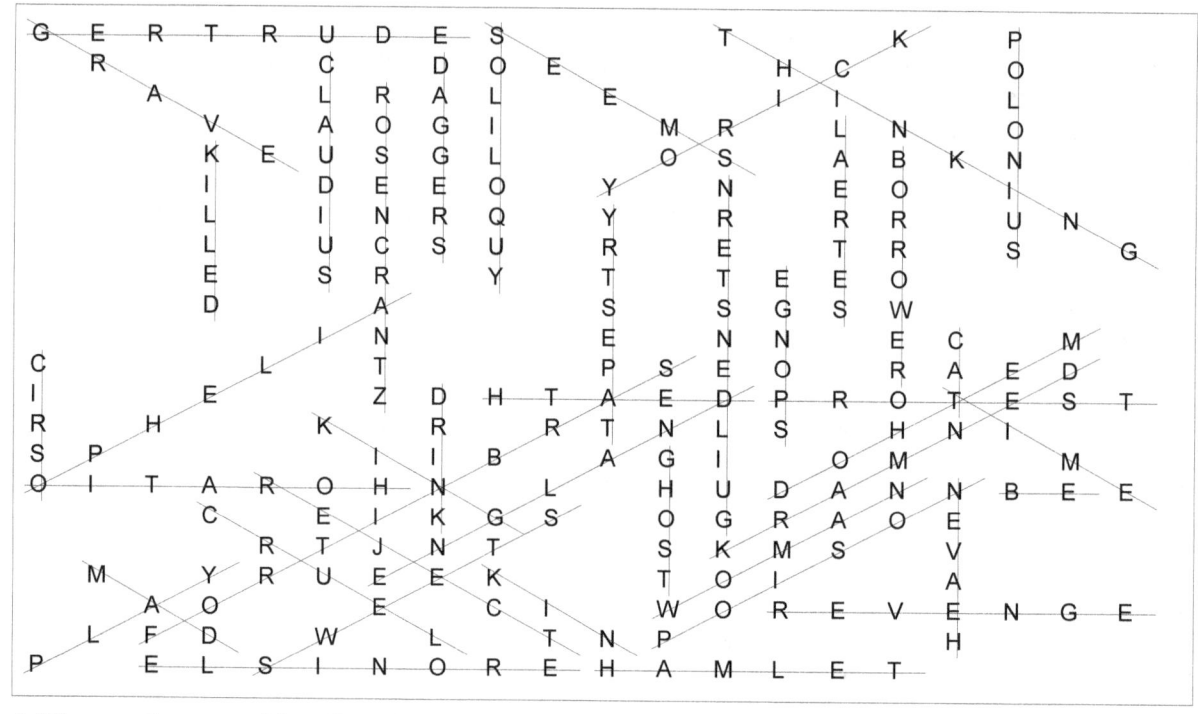

A little more than ____ & less than kind (3)
Alas, poor ____! I knew him, Horatio. (6)
Claudius wants Hamlet ____ when he reaches England (6)
Descriptive word Hamlet uses for Rosencrantz and Guildenstern (6)
Frailty, thy name is ____! (5)
Hamlet jumps into Ophelia's ____ (5)
Hamlet runs his sword through it, killing Polonius who was hiding there (8)
Hamlet sees the ____ of his father (5)
Hamlet wonders whether a miserable life is better than the unknown of ____ (5)
Hamlet's home (8)
Hamlet's mother (8)
Hamlet's uncle, the new King (8)
I must be ____ only to be kind. (5)
I will speak ____ to her, but use none. (7)
Laertes wants ____ for his father's death (7)
Leave her to ____/ And to those thorns that in her bosom lodge... (6)
Monologue by a character (9)
Neither a ____ nor a lender be. (8)
Old schoolmate and friend of Hamlet (7)
Ophelia's father (8)
Polonius & Laertes tell Ophelia to ____ Hamlet's affections (6)
Polonius thinks Hamlet has gone ____ because of

Ophelia's rejections (3)
Polonius' son (7)
Prince of Norway; wants to regain lands his father lost (10)
Rosencrantz and Guildenstern prepare to take Hamlet there (7)
Rosencrantz and ____ (12)
Sees his father's ghost and plans to get revenge for his father's murder (6)
She goes crazy and drowns (7)
Something is rotten in the state of ____. (7)
Tells Hamlet of the wager the King made on Hamlet's behalf (5)
The ____ is out of joint (4)
The ____ on Laertes sword kills Hamlet (6)
The ____ will mew and the dog will have his day. (3)
The ____'s the thing (4)
The ____, the ____'s to blame. (4)
The lady doth ____ too much, methinks. (7)
The queen dies after taking the poisoned ____ meant for Hamlet (5)
There is nothing either good or bad but ____ makes it so. (8)
Though this be madness, yet there is ____ in't. (6)
To ____ or not to ____ (2)
____ & Guildenstern (11)
____ to the ____ (6)
____, madam! Nay, it is. I know not ____. (5)

Hamlet Word Search 3

Words are placed backwards, forward, diagonally, up and down. Words listed below are included in the maze. Circle the hidden vocabulary words in the maze.

```
P X S O L I L O Q U Y T H I N K I N G M
X O G J R B V F M G Z L B N K H C R E L
M B L K F O F V J Y K M L K W C J E R R
G V Y O Q X S J H L J L L G C G M V T F
C B D R N T R E W O R R O B G B P E R M
W K M K X I Z R N D H S T N R L D N U G
W J L B X D U W S C J J H L Y M L G D P
G U I L D E N S T E R N D A J F F E E C
Y T C R T D G H C M R A C E P O H P E J
O C C L W B D J W X Z M N R R L E V D P
R G R E P K R M H A M L E T X C A T O Z
I Z U N G C I R X K M C I E Z R V Y H Q
C C E G M S N R D F I N Q S G B E S T H
K I L L E D K N J T B N C D Y B N C E K
T I T A J N A J C R I I G E E T E G M X
A O N N U M B E A T R M S A F N N J V B
P P S D O D J S N S W E E T S O M T C Y
E H D W F E I O O E F X E H P L A A H T
S E M F R J S U B T W S M S G D D K R K
T L Q V X I H C S O B M S C Z L T M R K
R I R N O O I T A R O H E L S I N O R E
Y A K P G H O S T P D A G G E R S C G F
```

BE
BORROWER
CAT
CLAUDIUS
CRUEL
DAGGERS
DEATH
DENMARK
DRINK
ELSINORE
ENGLAND

FORTINBRAS
GERTRUDE
GHOST
GRAVE
GUILDENSTERN
HAMLET
HEAVEN
HORATIO
KILLED
KIN
KING

LAERTES
MAD
METHOD
OPHELIA
OSRIC
PLAY
POISON
POLONIUS
PROTEST
REJECT
REVENGE

ROSENCRANTZ
SEEMS
SOLILOQUY
SPONGE
SWEETS
TAPESTRY
THINKING
TIME
WOMAN
YORICK

Hamlet Word Search 3 Answer Key

Words are placed backwards, forward, diagonally, up and down. Words listed below are included in the maze. Circle the hidden vocabulary words in the maze.

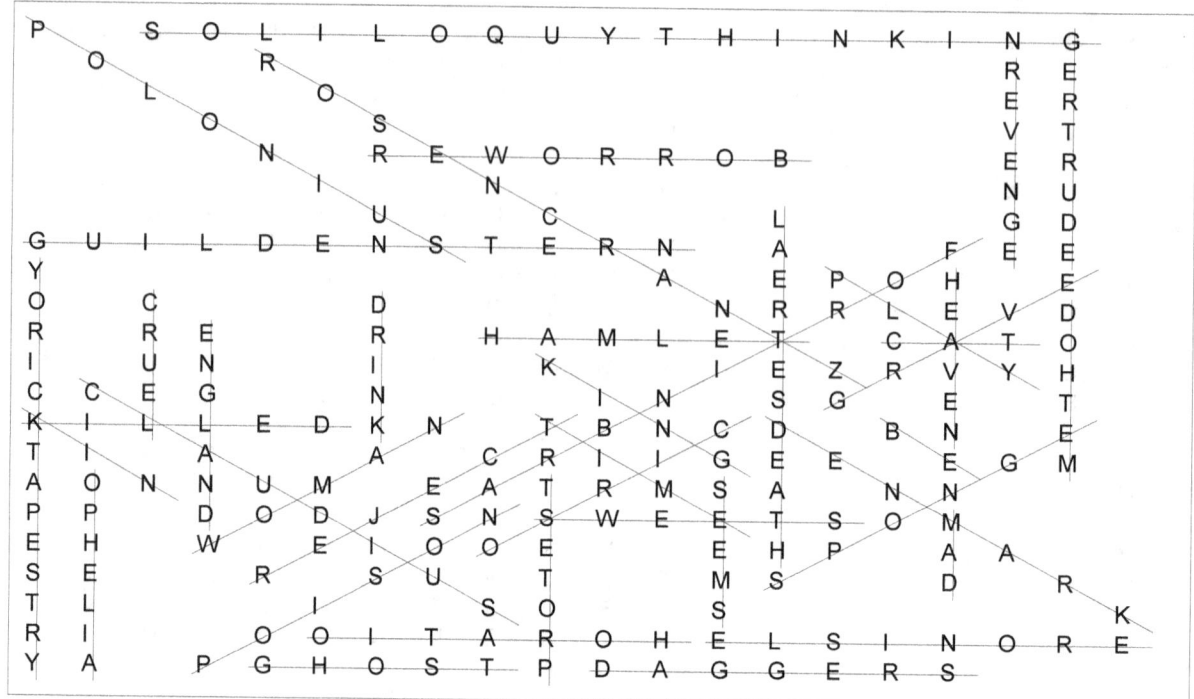

BE	FORTINBRAS	LAERTES	ROSENCRANTZ
BORROWER	GERTRUDE	MAD	SEEMS
CAT	GHOST	METHOD	SOLILOQUY
CLAUDIUS	GRAVE	OPHELIA	SPONGE
CRUEL	GUILDENSTERN	OSRIC	SWEETS
DAGGERS	HAMLET	PLAY	TAPESTRY
DEATH	HEAVEN	POISON	THINKING
DENMARK	HORATIO	POLONIUS	TIME
DRINK	KILLED	PROTEST	WOMAN
ELSINORE	KIN	REJECT	YORICK
ENGLAND	KING	REVENGE	

Hamlet Word Search 4

Words are placed backwards, forward, diagonally, up and down. Words listed below are included in the maze. Circle the hidden vocabulary words in the maze.

```
C L A U D I U S C R U E L C H S E K G N
Z Z B E A H T N E A V D A B E W L I U Y
M T A J M X C V C A T E E J A E S N I L
Z T M X S E E B R N S N R K V E I P L M
H F J T G N J G K S E M T B E T N O D V
H F R N G E E H A K E A E R N S O L E L
N V O E L L R A B M R S T M B R O N N
X P S Q N S B T N M S K Y Z E C E N S F
S Y E P K N E H R T L V P F T B D I T V
T F N G I R N I B U A E D R H Q A U E J
G Y C T L C G N G J D P T B O Q G S R F
L F R Q L N L K P Q X E E K D T G F N X
C O A B E X A I M O V L P S T T E T H Z
F C N F D N N N Q H I K K T B R S H Z
R C T D J P D G W C V S N J P R S R T M
X D Z Y V W R A B Q D I O K B J Y E H P
W T S N R V I K J B R P C N X T M W F C
F X D G H L V Z P D W I N M Q N J O I P
K P X H E B N G L Q R S H E F A D R K G
J T L H N D Z Y A O W B M M Z M S R I J
Y Z P N Q L H F Y L O I T A R O H O N R
S O L I L O Q U Y F T S O H G W J B G K
```

BE	FORTINBRAS	LAERTES	ROSENCRANTZ
BORROWER	GERTRUDE	MAD	SEEMS
CAT	GHOST	METHOD	SOLILOQUY
CLAUDIUS	GRAVE	OPHELIA	SPONGE
CRUEL	GUILDENSTERN	OSRIC	SWEETS
DAGGERS	HAMLET	PLAY	TAPESTRY
DEATH	HEAVEN	POISON	THINKING
DENMARK	HORATIO	POLONIUS	TIME
DRINK	KILLED	PROTEST	WOMAN
ELSINORE	KIN	REJECT	YORICK
ENGLAND	KING	REVENGE	

Hamlet Word Search 4 Answer Key

Words are placed backwards, forward, diagonally, up and down. Words listed below are included in the maze. Circle the hidden vocabulary words in the maze.

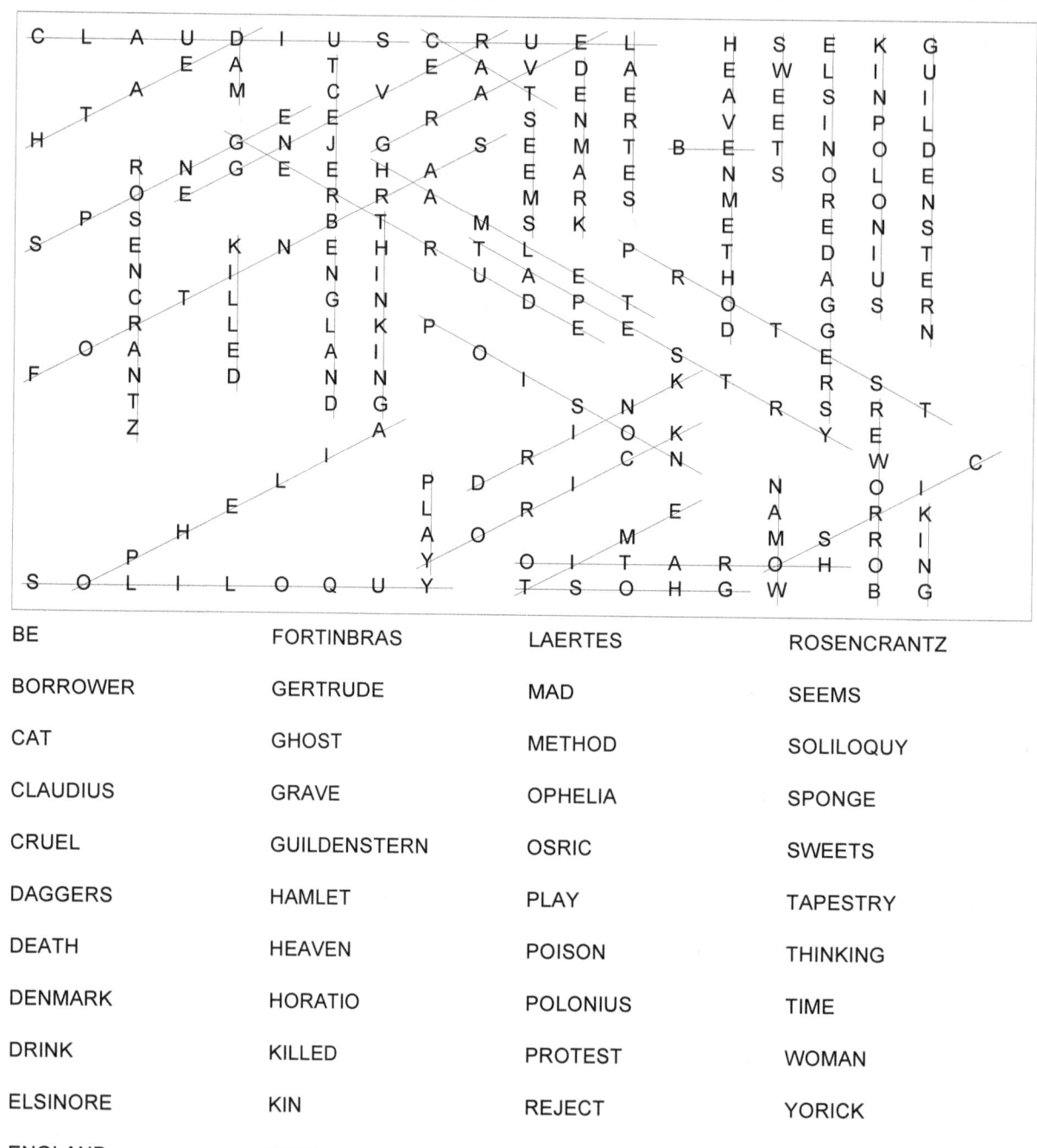

BE	FORTINBRAS	LAERTES	ROSENCRANTZ
BORROWER	GERTRUDE	MAD	SEEMS
CAT	GHOST	METHOD	SOLILOQUY
CLAUDIUS	GRAVE	OPHELIA	SPONGE
CRUEL	GUILDENSTERN	OSRIC	SWEETS
DAGGERS	HAMLET	PLAY	TAPESTRY
DEATH	HEAVEN	POISON	THINKING
DENMARK	HORATIO	POLONIUS	TIME
DRINK	KILLED	PROTEST	WOMAN
ELSINORE	KIN	REJECT	YORICK
ENGLAND	KING	REVENGE	

Hamlet Crossword 1

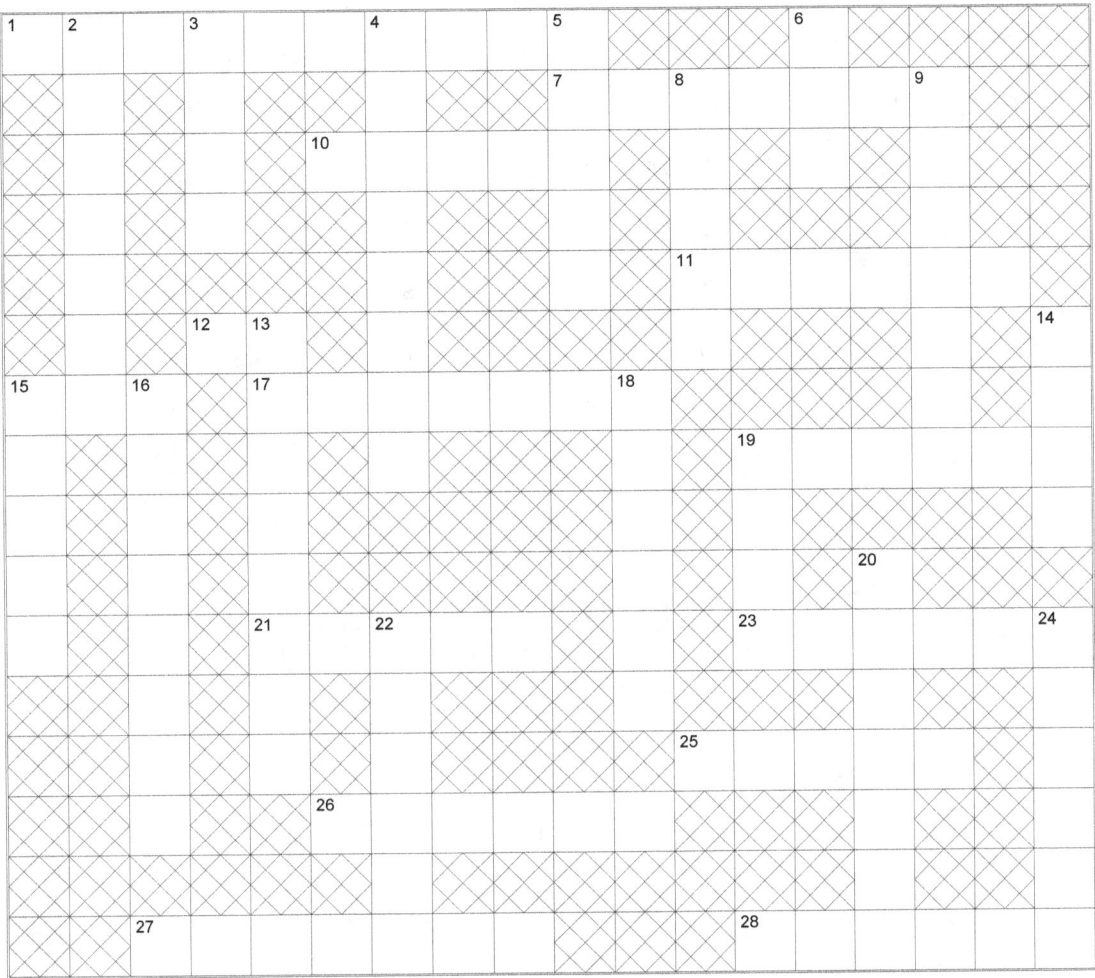

Across
1. Prince of Norway; wants to regain lands his father lost
7. Rosencrantz and Guildenstern prepare to take Hamlet there
10. Hamlet jumps into Ophelia's ____
11. Descriptive word Hamlet uses for Rosencrantz and Guildenstern
12. To ____ or not to ____
15. The ____ will mew and the dog will have his day.
17. Polonius' son
19. The ____ on Laertes sword kills Hamlet
21. Tells Hamlet of the wager the King made on Hamlet's behalf
23. Alas, poor ____! I knew him, Horatio.
25. Hamlet wonders whether a miserable life is better than the unknown of ____
26. Leave her to ____/ And to those thorns that in her bosom lodge...
27. Old schoolmate and friend of Hamlet
28. Though this be madness, yet there is ____ in't.

Down
2. She goes crazy and drowns
3. The ____ is out of joint
4. Neither a ____ nor a lender be.
5. ____, madam! Nay, it is. I know not ____.
6. Polonius thinks Hamlet has gone ____ because of Ophelia's rejections
8. Hamlet sees the ____ of his father
9. I will speak ____ to her, but use none.
13. Hamlet's home
14. The ____, the ____'s to blame.
15. I must be ____ only to be kind.
16. Hamlet runs his sword through it, killing Polonius who was hiding there
18. ____ to the ____
19. The ____'s the thing
20. The lady doth ____ too much, methinks.
22. Polonius & Laertes tell Ophelia to ____ Hamlet's affections
24. Claudius wants Hamlet ____ when he reaches England

Hamlet Crossword 1 Answer Key

	1 F	2 O	3 R	T	I	4 N	B	R	A	5 S			6 M		
		P	I			O			7 E	8 N	G	L	A	9 N	D
		H	M		10 G	R	A	V	E	H		D		A	
		E	E		R				M	O				G	
		L			O				S	11 S	P	O	N	G	E
		I	12 B	13 E	W					T				E	14 K
15 C	16 A	17 T	L	A	E	R	T	E	18 S					R	I
R	T		S	R					W	19 P	O	I	S	O	N
U	A		I						E	L					G
E	P		N						E	A		20 P			
L	E		21 O	22 S	R	I	C		T	23 Y	O	R	I	C	24 K
	T		R	E					S			O			I
	R		E	J				25 D	E	A	T	H			L
	Y		26 H	E	A	V	E	N				E			L
				C								S			E
			27 H	O	R	A	T	I	O		28 M	E	T	H	O	D

Across

1. Prince of Norway; wants to regain lands his father lost
7. Rosencrantz and Guildenstern prepare to take Hamlet there
10. Hamlet jumps into Ophelia's ____
11. Descriptive word Hamlet uses for Rosencrantz and Guildenstern
12. To ____ or not to ____
15. The ____ will mew and the dog will have his day.
17. Polonius' son
19. The ____ on Laertes sword kills Hamlet
21. Tells Hamlet of the wager the King made on Hamlet's behalf
23. Alas, poor ____! I knew him, Horatio.
25. Hamlet wonders whether a miserable life is better than the unknown of ____
26. Leave her to ____ / And to those thorns that in her bosom lodge...
27. Old schoolmate and friend of Hamlet
28. Though this be madness, yet there is ____ in't.

Down

2. She goes crazy and drowns
3. The ____ is out of joint
4. Neither a ____ nor a lender be.
5. ____, madam! Nay, it is. I know not ____.
6. Polonius thinks Hamlet has gone ____ because of Ophelia's rejections
8. Hamlet sees the ____ of his father
9. I will speak ____ to her, but use none.
13. Hamlet's home
14. The ____, the ____'s to blame.
15. I must be ____ only to be kind.
16. Hamlet runs his sword through it, killing Polonius who was hiding there
18. ____ to the ____
19. The ____'s the thing
20. The lady doth ____ too much, methinks.
22. Polonius & Laertes tell Ophelia to ____ Hamlet's affections
24. Claudius wants Hamlet ____ when he reaches England

Hamlet Crossword 2

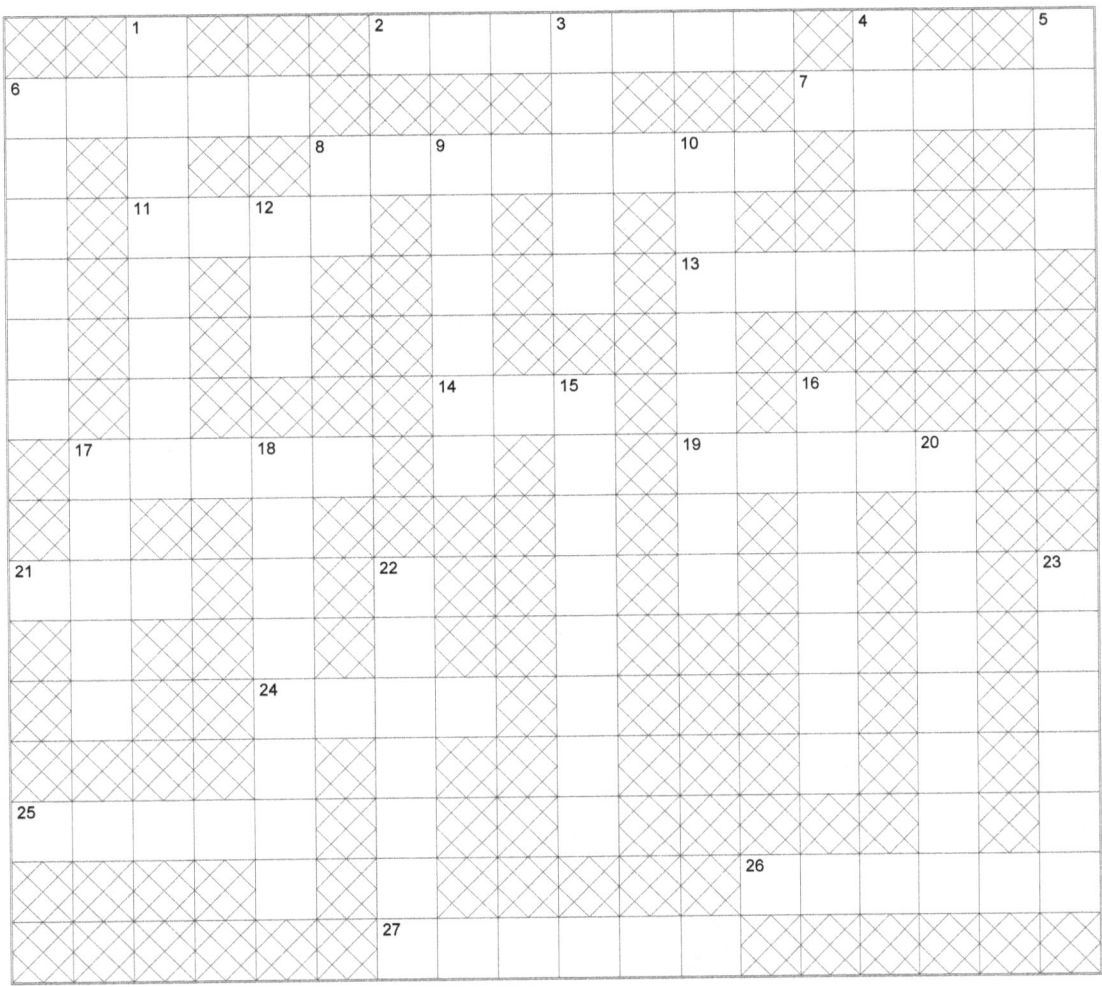

Across
2. I will speak ____ to her, but use none.
6. ____, madam! Nay, it is. I know not ____.
7. I must be ____ only to be kind.
8. Neither a ____ nor a lender be.
11. The ____ is out of joint
13. ____ to the ____
14. The ____ will mew and the dog will have his day.
17. Hamlet wonders whether a miserable life is better than the unknown of ____
19. Tells Hamlet of the wager the King made on Hamlet's behalf
21. A little more than ____ & less than kind
24. The ____, the ____'s to blame.
25. Frailty, thy name is ____!
26. The ____ on Laertes sword kills Hamlet
27. Claudius wants Hamlet ____ when he reaches England

Down
1. Hamlet's mother
3. Hamlet sees the ____ of his father
4. Hamlet jumps into Ophelia's ____
5. The ____'s the thing
6. Descriptive word Hamlet uses for Rosencrantz and Guildenstern
8. To ____ or not to ____
9. Polonius & Laertes tell Ophelia to ____ Hamlet's affections
10. Hamlet's home
12. Polonius thinks Hamlet has gone ____ because of Ophelia's rejections
15. Hamlet runs his sword through it, killing Polonius who was hiding there
16. The lady doth ____ too much, methinks.
17. The queen dies after taking the poisoned ____ meant for Hamlet
18. There is nothing either good or bad but ____ makes it so.
20. Hamlet's uncle, the new King
22. Something is rotten in the state of ____.
23. Leave her to ____/ And to those thorns that in her bosom lodge...

Hamlet Crossword 2 Answer Key

			1 G			2 D	A	3 G	G	E	R	S		4 G		5 P
6 S	E	E	M	S				H					7 C	R	U	E	L
P		R			8 B	O	9 R	R	O	W	10 E	R		A		A
O	11 T	I	12 M	E		E		S			L			V		Y
N	R		A			J		T		13 S	W	E	E	T	S	
G	U		D		14 C	A	15 T		16 P		I					
E	17 D	18 E	A	T	H		T		19 O	S	R	I	20 C		
	R		H				A		R		O		L			
21 K	I	N		22 D		E		E		T		A	23 H
N		I	N		E		S		E		U		E
	K		24 K	I	N	G		T		S		D		A
			I		M		R		T		I		V
25 W	O	M	A	N		A		Y				U		E
			G	R					26 P	O	I	S	O	N
			27 K	I	L	L	E	D

Across
2. I will speak ____ to her, but use none.
6. ____, madam! Nay, it is. I know not ____.
7. I must be ____ only to be kind.
8. Neither a ____ nor a lender be.
11. The ____ is out of joint
13. ____ to the ____
14. The ____ will mew and the dog will have his day.
17. Hamlet wonders whether a miserable life is better than the unknown of ____
19. Tells Hamlet of the wager the King made on Hamlet's behalf
21. A little more than ____ & less than kind
24. The ____, the ____'s to blame.
25. Frailty, thy name is ____!
26. The ____ on Laertes sword kills Hamlet
27. Claudius wants Hamlet ____ when he reaches England

Down
1. Hamlet's mother
3. Hamlet sees the ____ of his father
4. Hamlet jumps into Ophelia's ____
5. The ____'s the thing
6. Descriptive word Hamlet uses for Rosencrantz and Guildenstern
8. To ____ or not to ____
9. Polonius & Laertes tell Ophelia to ____ Hamlet's affections
10. Hamlet's home
12. Polonius thinks Hamlet has gone ____ because of Ophelia's rejections
15. Hamlet runs his sword through it, killing Polonius who was hiding there
16. The lady doth ____ too much, methinks.
17. The queen dies after taking the poisoned ____ meant for Hamlet
18. There is nothing either good or bad but ____ makes it so.
20. Hamlet's uncle, the new King
22. Something is rotten in the state of ____.
23. Leave her to ____/ And to those thorns that in her bosom lodge...

Hamlet Crossword 3

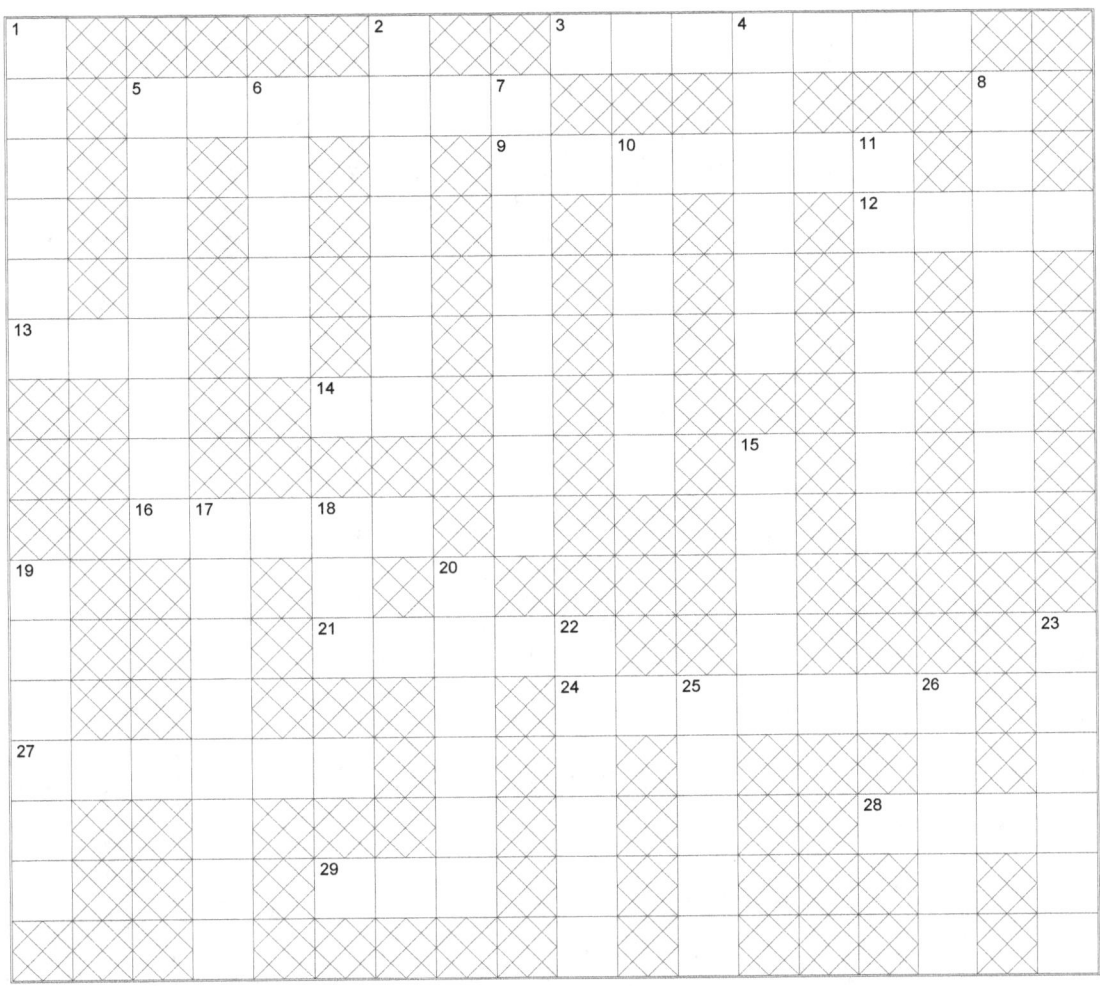

Across
3. Something is rotten in the state of ____.
5. The lady doth ____ too much, methinks.
9. Old schoolmate and friend of Hamlet
12. The ____'s the thing
13. A little more than ____ & less than kind
14. To ____ or not to ____
16. ____, madam! Nay, it is. I know not ____.
21. Hamlet wonders whether a miserable life is better than the unknown of ____
24. Rosencrantz and Guildenstern prepare to take Hamlet there
27. Descriptive word Hamlet uses for Rosencrantz and Guildenstern
28. The ____ is out of joint
29. The ____ will mew and the dog will have his day.

Down
1. Alas, poor ____! I knew him, Horatio.
2. Laertes wants ____ for his father's death
4. Though this be madness, yet there is ____ in't.
5. Ophelia's father
6. Tells Hamlet of the wager the King made on Hamlet's behalf
7. There is nothing either good or bad but ____ makes it so.
8. Hamlet's uncle, the new King
10. Polonius & Laertes tell Ophelia to ____ Hamlet's affections
11. She goes crazy and drowns
15. I must be ____ only to be kind.
17. Hamlet's home
18. Polonius thinks Hamlet has gone ____ because of Ophelia's rejections
19. The ____ on Laertes sword kills Hamlet
20. Sees his father's ghost and plans to get revenge for his father's murder
22. Leave her to ____/ And to those thorns that in her bosom lodge...
23. ____ to the ____
25. Hamlet jumps into Ophelia's ____
26. The queen dies after taking the poisoned ____ meant for Hamlet

Hamlet Crossword 3 Answer Key

Across
3. Something is rotten in the state of ____.
5. The lady doth ____ too much, methinks.
9. Old schoolmate and friend of Hamlet
12. The ____'s the thing
13. A little more than ____ & less than kind
14. To ____ or not to ____
16. ____, madam! Nay, it is. I know not ____.
21. Hamlet wonders whether a miserable life is better than the unknown of ____
24. Rosencrantz and Guildenstern prepare to take Hamlet there
27. Descriptive word Hamlet uses for Rosencrantz and Guildenstern
28. The ____ is out of joint
29. The ____ will mew and the dog will have his day.

Down
1. Alas, poor ____! I knew him, Horatio.
2. Laertes wants ____ for his father's death
4. Though this be madness, yet there is ____ in't.
5. Ophelia's father
6. Tells Hamlet of the wager the King made on Hamlet's behalf
7. There is nothing either good or bad but ____ makes it so.
8. Hamlet's uncle, the new King
10. Polonius & Laertes tell Ophelia to ____ Hamlet's affections
11. She goes crazy and drowns
15. I must be ____ only to be kind.
17. Hamlet's home
18. Polonius thinks Hamlet has gone ____ because of Ophelia's rejections
19. The ____ on Laertes sword kills Hamlet
20. Sees his father's ghost and plans to get revenge for his father's murder
22. Leave her to ____/ And to those thorns that in her bosom lodge...
23. ____ to the ____
25. Hamlet jumps into Ophelia's ____
26. The queen dies after taking the poisoned ____ meant for Hamlet

Hamlet Crossword 4

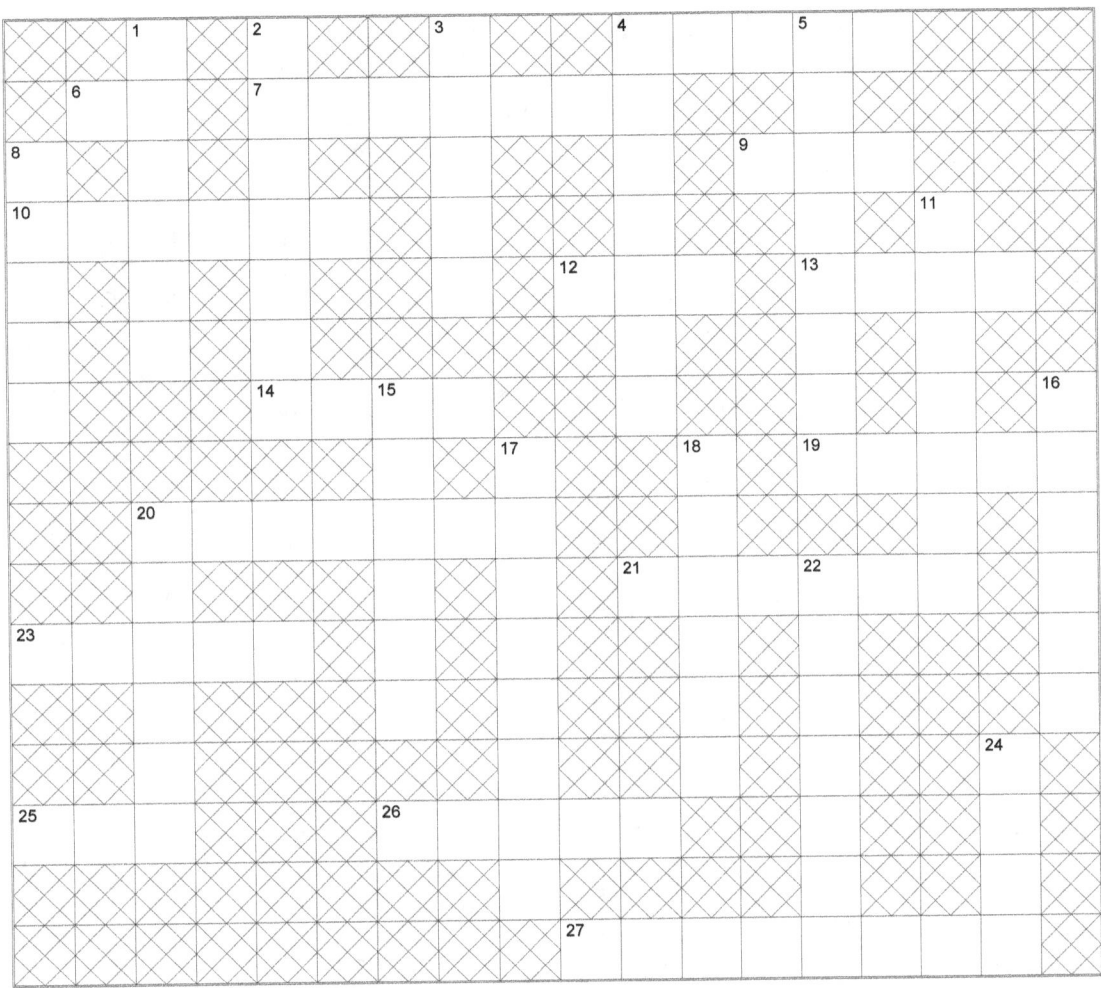

Across

4. Hamlet wonders whether a miserable life is better than the unknown of ____
6. To ____ or not to ____
7. Laertes wants ____ for his father's death
9. A little more than ____ & less than kind
10. ____ to the ____
12. Polonius thinks Hamlet has gone ____ because of Ophelia's rejections
13. The ____, the ____'s to blame.
14. The ____ is out of joint
19. Hamlet jumps into Ophelia's ____
20. Old schoolmate and friend of Hamlet
21. Claudius wants Hamlet ____ when he reaches England
23. Frailty, thy name is ____!
25. The ____ will mew and the dog will have his day.
26. I must be ____ only to be kind.
27. Hamlet runs his sword through it, killing Polonius who was hiding there

Down

1. Polonius & Laertes tell Ophelia to ____ Hamlet's affections
2. The lady doth ____ too much, methinks.
3. ____, madam! Nay, it is. I know not ____.
4. Something is rotten in the state of ____.
5. There is nothing either good or bad but ____ makes it so.
8. Tells Hamlet of the wager the King made on Hamlet's behalf
11. Rosencrantz and Guildenstern prepare to take Hamlet there
15. Though this be madness, yet there is ____ in't.
16. Leave her to ____/ And to those thorns that in her bosom lodge...
17. Ophelia's father
18. The ____ on Laertes sword kills Hamlet
20. Sees his father's ghost and plans to get revenge for his father's murder
22. Polonius' son
24. The ____'s the thing

Hamlet Crossword 4 Answer Key

	1 R	2 P		3 S		4 D	5 T		
6 B	E	7 R	E	V	E	N	G	E	
8 O		J	O		E		N	9 K	I	N
10 S	W	E	E	T	S		M	N		11 E
R		C	E			12 M	A	D	13 K	I	N	G
I		T	S				R		I		G
C		14 T	15 I	M	E		K		N		16 H
		E			17 P	18 P	19 G	R	A	V	E
	20 H	O	R	A	T	I	O		N		A
	A		H		L	21 K	22 L	I	L	E	D
23 W	O	M	A	N		O	S	A		E
	L		D		N	R	T		24 P
	E		25 C	A	T	I	26 C	R	U	E	L
				S			27 T	A	P	E	S	T	R	Y

Across

4. Hamlet wonders whether a miserable life is better than the unknown of ____
6. To ____ or not to ____
7. Laertes wants ____ for his father's death
9. A little more than ____ & less than kind
10. ____ to the ____
12. Polonius thinks Hamlet has gone ____ because of Ophelia's rejections
13. The ____, the ____'s to blame.
14. The ____ is out of joint
19. Hamlet jumps into Ophelia's ____
20. Old schoolmate and friend of Hamlet
21. Claudius wants Hamlet ____ when he reaches England
23. Frailty, thy name is ____!
25. The ____ will mew and the dog will have his day.
26. I must be ____ only to be kind.
27. Hamlet runs his sword through it, killing Polonius who was hiding there

Down

1. Polonius & Laertes tell Ophelia to ____ Hamlet's affections
2. The lady doth ____ too much, methinks.
3. ____, madam! Nay, it is. I know not ____.
4. Something is rotten in the state of ____.
5. There is nothing either good or bad but ____ makes it so.
8. Tells Hamlet of the wager the King made on Hamlet's behalf
11. Rosencrantz and Guildenstern prepare to take Hamlet there
15. Though this be madness, yet there is ____ in't.
16. Leave her to ____/ And to those thorns that in her bosom lodge...
17. Ophelia's father
18. The ____ on Laertes sword kills Hamlet
20. Sees his father's ghost and plans to get revenge for his father's murder
22. Polonius' son
24. The ____'s the thing

Hamlet

BE	POLONIUS	CLAUDIUS	CAT	DENMARK
GHOST	KILLED	ELSINORE	LAERTES	REJECT
SOLILOQUY	BORROWER	FREE SPACE	KING	POISON
KIN	OSRIC	HAMLET	DEATH	MAD
TAPESTRY	TIME	OPHELIA	DAGGERS	METHOD

Hamlet

WOMAN	REVENGE	SWEETS	HEAVEN	SEEMS
CRUEL	DRINK	ROSENCRANTZ	GERTRUDE	PROTEST
GRAVE	YORICK	FREE SPACE	FORTINBRAS	PLAY
ENGLAND	HORATIO	GUILDENSTERN	METHOD	DAGGERS
OPHELIA	TIME	TAPESTRY	MAD	DEATH

Hamlet

TIME	SWEETS	PROTEST	BORROWER	OPHELIA
WOMAN	HAMLET	REVENGE	KIN	HEAVEN
CRUEL	SPONGE	FREE SPACE	HORATIO	PLAY
CAT	ROSENCRANTZ	ELSINORE	CLAUDIUS	DRINK
MAD	TAPESTRY	POISON	REJECT	YORICK

Hamlet

ENGLAND	DEATH	LAERTES	METHOD	GUILDENSTERN
DAGGERS	OSRIC	KING	GRAVE	THINKING
FORTINBRAS	POLONIUS	FREE SPACE	DENMARK	GERTRUDE
KILLED	SEEMS	BE	YORICK	REJECT
POISON	TAPESTRY	MAD	DRINK	CLAUDIUS

Hamlet

SOLILOQUY	CLAUDIUS	DRINK	DENMARK	SWEETS
PLAY	METHOD	REJECT	GUILDENSTERN	TAPESTRY
OSRIC	MAD	FREE SPACE	PROTEST	YORICK
KILLED	LAERTES	SPONGE	FORTINBRAS	ELSINORE
POISON	REVENGE	DEATH	HEAVEN	OPHELIA

Hamlet

BORROWER	SEEMS	DAGGERS	HORATIO	TIME
CAT	GHOST	KING	KIN	POLONIUS
ROSENCRANTZ	WOMAN	FREE SPACE	CRUEL	THINKING
GERTRUDE	HAMLET	BE	OPHELIA	HEAVEN
DEATH	REVENGE	POISON	ELSINORE	FORTINBRAS

Hamlet

PROTEST	WOMAN	OSRIC	ELSINORE	SWEETS
YORICK	ROSENCRANTZ	SOLILOQUY	LAERTES	GHOST
BORROWER	DRINK	FREE SPACE	HEAVEN	REVENGE
KILLED	DENMARK	FORTINBRAS	GERTRUDE	CLAUDIUS
DEATH	OPHELIA	METHOD	POLONIUS	TIME

Hamlet

SPONGE	GRAVE	HAMLET	ENGLAND	GUILDENSTERN
POISON	PLAY	BE	KIN	CRUEL
CAT	HORATIO	FREE SPACE	KING	SEEMS
TAPESTRY	REJECT	THINKING	TIME	POLONIUS
METHOD	OPHELIA	DEATH	CLAUDIUS	GERTRUDE

Hamlet

CRUEL	KIN	FORTINBRAS	POISON	PROTEST
DRINK	REVENGE	SEEMS	WOMAN	DEATH
DENMARK	GHOST	FREE SPACE	TIME	METHOD
CAT	GRAVE	BORROWER	ROSENCRANTZ	KING
CLAUDIUS	OSRIC	TAPESTRY	BE	PLAY

Hamlet

MAD	SOLILOQUY	HAMLET	GERTRUDE	OPHELIA
YORICK	DAGGERS	SWEETS	REJECT	SPONGE
KILLED	HEAVEN	FREE SPACE	HORATIO	ENGLAND
ELSINORE	THINKING	GUILDENSTERN	PLAY	BE
TAPESTRY	OSRIC	CLAUDIUS	KING	ROSENCRANTZ

Hamlet

SWEETS	BORROWER	POISON	GUILDENSTERN	YORICK
KILLED	KIN	WOMAN	DRINK	PROTEST
FORTINBRAS	GERTRUDE	FREE SPACE	MAD	THINKING
METHOD	HAMLET	SEEMS	DENMARK	OPHELIA
ROSENCRANTZ	REVENGE	LAERTES	POLONIUS	CLAUDIUS

Hamlet

GRAVE	DAGGERS	CAT	BE	HEAVEN
PLAY	SOLILOQUY	TIME	OSRIC	DEATH
CRUEL	SPONGE	FREE SPACE	ENGLAND	ELSINORE
HORATIO	TAPESTRY	REJECT	CLAUDIUS	POLONIUS
LAERTES	REVENGE	ROSENCRANTZ	OPHELIA	DENMARK

Hamlet

KIN	PROTEST	CRUEL	POISON	OPHELIA
CLAUDIUS	SPONGE	SWEETS	GERTRUDE	FORTINBRAS
BORROWER	SEEMS	FREE SPACE	METHOD	HEAVEN
DRINK	POLONIUS	DEATH	TIME	YORICK
ROSENCRANTZ	KING	DENMARK	REJECT	HORATIO

Hamlet

THINKING	DAGGERS	TAPESTRY	GHOST	HAMLET
SOLILOQUY	BE	REVENGE	LAERTES	OSRIC
ENGLAND	ELSINORE	FREE SPACE	GUILDENSTERN	CAT
GRAVE	PLAY	KILLED	HORATIO	REJECT
DENMARK	KING	ROSENCRANTZ	YORICK	TIME

Hamlet

FORTINBRAS	POISON	POLONIUS	BE	REJECT
ENGLAND	SOLILOQUY	METHOD	LAERTES	GHOST
DAGGERS	MAD	FREE SPACE	REVENGE	HAMLET
WOMAN	DRINK	OSRIC	TIME	GRAVE
CLAUDIUS	KING	DENMARK	TAPESTRY	PROTEST

Hamlet

BORROWER	SPONGE	HORATIO	CAT	KIN
YORICK	KILLED	ROSENCRANTZ	PLAY	ELSINORE
DEATH	CRUEL	FREE SPACE	OPHELIA	GERTRUDE
SWEETS	GUILDENSTERN	SEEMS	PROTEST	TAPESTRY
DENMARK	KING	CLAUDIUS	GRAVE	TIME

Hamlet

SWEETS	SPONGE	POISON	DRINK	GERTRUDE
FORTINBRAS	CLAUDIUS	BE	LAERTES	REVENGE
TIME	HEAVEN	FREE SPACE	GHOST	REJECT
PROTEST	PLAY	DEATH	YORICK	DAGGERS
CAT	WOMAN	POLONIUS	ELSINORE	KING

Hamlet

KIN	CRUEL	TAPESTRY	GUILDENSTERN	HAMLET
SOLILOQUY	KILLED	ENGLAND	OSRIC	BORROWER
SEEMS	MAD	FREE SPACE	ROSENCRANTZ	DENMARK
THINKING	GRAVE	HORATIO	KING	ELSINORE
POLONIUS	WOMAN	CAT	DAGGERS	YORICK

Hamlet

SWEETS	BE	LAERTES	CRUEL	DEATH
DRINK	POISON	OPHELIA	HORATIO	OSRIC
DENMARK	DAGGERS	FREE SPACE	SEEMS	THINKING
CLAUDIUS	ENGLAND	BORROWER	WOMAN	ROSENCRANTZ
TAPESTRY	KIN	GERTRUDE	FORTINBRAS	HAMLET

Hamlet

POLONIUS	PROTEST	KILLED	GHOST	GUILDENSTERN
PLAY	TIME	MAD	METHOD	HEAVEN
REVENGE	ELSINORE	FREE SPACE	SOLILOQUY	YORICK
SPONGE	KING	REJECT	HAMLET	FORTINBRAS
GERTRUDE	KIN	TAPESTRY	ROSENCRANTZ	WOMAN

Hamlet

TIME	BE	FORTINBRAS	METHOD	CAT
OPHELIA	ELSINORE	SWEETS	DAGGERS	KILLED
LAERTES	CLAUDIUS	FREE SPACE	POISON	DENMARK
SPONGE	MAD	HEAVEN	REVENGE	POLONIUS
PLAY	CRUEL	PROTEST	DRINK	WOMAN

Hamlet

OSRIC	HORATIO	GRAVE	HAMLET	REJECT
GUILDENSTERN	GERTRUDE	SEEMS	SOLILOQUY	TAPESTRY
GHOST	THINKING	FREE SPACE	DEATH	ENGLAND
YORICK	KIN	ROSENCRANTZ	WOMAN	DRINK
PROTEST	CRUEL	PLAY	POLONIUS	REVENGE

Hamlet

OPHELIA	PLAY	CRUEL	DENMARK	SOLILOQUY
MAD	CAT	YORICK	SWEETS	WOMAN
ROSENCRANTZ	GERTRUDE	FREE SPACE	DEATH	GRAVE
KIN	BE	GHOST	TAPESTRY	KING
FORTINBRAS	TIME	GUILDENSTERN	HEAVEN	SPONGE

Hamlet

PROTEST	THINKING	ENGLAND	HORATIO	DRINK
CLAUDIUS	SEEMS	KILLED	POISON	HAMLET
OSRIC	DAGGERS	FREE SPACE	ELSINORE	BORROWER
REJECT	LAERTES	POLONIUS	SPONGE	HEAVEN
GUILDENSTERN	TIME	FORTINBRAS	KING	TAPESTRY

56
Copyrighted

Hamlet

CRUEL	CLAUDIUS	GHOST	GUILDENSTERN	PROTEST
TAPESTRY	YORICK	REJECT	HEAVEN	BE
DENMARK	GERTRUDE	FREE SPACE	PLAY	OSRIC
CAT	ELSINORE	SWEETS	KIN	ENGLAND
WOMAN	KILLED	KING	THINKING	HORATIO

Hamlet

DRINK	TIME	REVENGE	DAGGERS	GRAVE
ROSENCRANTZ	DEATH	POISON	SPONGE	FORTINBRAS
POLONIUS	OPHELIA	FREE SPACE	BORROWER	METHOD
SOLILOQUY	SEEMS	HAMLET	HORATIO	THINKING
KING	KILLED	WOMAN	ENGLAND	KIN

Hamlet

ELSINORE	CRUEL	FORTINBRAS	OSRIC	GUILDENSTERN
HORATIO	POISON	PROTEST	SWEETS	GERTRUDE
MAD	KIN	FREE SPACE	TIME	ROSENCRANTZ
DENMARK	KILLED	PLAY	GRAVE	BE
OPHELIA	METHOD	HAMLET	GHOST	LAERTES

Hamlet

CLAUDIUS	POLONIUS	YORICK	THINKING	CAT
HEAVEN	SPONGE	REVENGE	SEEMS	REJECT
KING	SOLILOQUY	FREE SPACE	DAGGERS	BORROWER
DRINK	TAPESTRY	ENGLAND	LAERTES	GHOST
HAMLET	METHOD	OPHELIA	BE	GRAVE

Hamlet

DENMARK	HEAVEN	LAERTES	ENGLAND	HORATIO
FORTINBRAS	PLAY	OPHELIA	KIN	CLAUDIUS
BE	GUILDENSTERN	FREE SPACE	MAD	POISON
BORROWER	CAT	DAGGERS	REJECT	SWEETS
DEATH	THINKING	PROTEST	SPONGE	TAPESTRY

Hamlet

TIME	KILLED	HAMLET	ROSENCRANTZ	DRINK
ELSINORE	WOMAN	SEEMS	OSRIC	GHOST
SOLILOQUY	CRUEL	FREE SPACE	GRAVE	KING
GERTRUDE	REVENGE	METHOD	TAPESTRY	SPONGE
PROTEST	THINKING	DEATH	SWEETS	REJECT

Hamlet

DRINK	THINKING	ELSINORE	TIME	DAGGERS
DENMARK	CRUEL	FORTINBRAS	REVENGE	ROSENCRANTZ
CLAUDIUS	KIN	FREE SPACE	DEATH	SPONGE
BE	PLAY	SEEMS	PROTEST	ENGLAND
HAMLET	OSRIC	GHOST	OPHELIA	LAERTES

Hamlet

SOLILOQUY	GRAVE	SWEETS	BORROWER	HORATIO
TAPESTRY	MAD	WOMAN	METHOD	POISON
KING	YORICK	FREE SPACE	KILLED	GERTRUDE
POLONIUS	GUILDENSTERN	REJECT	LAERTES	OPHELIA
GHOST	OSRIC	HAMLET	ENGLAND	PROTEST

Hamlet Vocabulary Word List

No.	Word	Clue/Definition
1.	ABATEMENTS	Reduction in amount, degree, or intensity
2.	AFFLICT	To inflict grievous physical or mental suffering on
3.	ALOOF	Distant physically or emotionally
4.	AMBIGUOUS	Open to more than one interpretation
5.	APPURTENANCE	Something added to another, more important thing; an appendage
6.	BASE	The lowest or bottom part
7.	BESEECH	To address an earnest or urgent request to
8.	CARNAL	Of or relating to the body or flesh; bodily
9.	CHURLISH	Difficult to work with
10.	COMMINGLED	Mixed together
11.	CONJURATION	Influence or effect by a supernatural power
12.	CONTAGION	A harmful, corrupting influence
13.	CONTRIVE	To plan with cleverness or ingenuity; scheme
14.	CONVOCATION	Assembly
15.	DISCORD	Tension or strife
16.	DISCRETION	Ability or power to decide responsibly
17.	DIVULGING	Becoming known
18.	ENTREAT	To make an earnest request of
19.	EPITAPH	An inscription on a tombstone in memory of the one buried there
20.	EXTOLMENT	High praise
21.	FELICITY	Great happiness; bliss
22.	FILIAL	The relationship of child or offspring to parent
23.	IMMINENT	About to occur; impending
24.	INVULNERABLE	Immune to attack; impregnable; impossible to damage, injure, or wound
25.	KNAVISH	Unprincipled
26.	MALICIOUS	Spiteful
27.	PARAGON	A model of excellence or perfection
28.	PERDITION	Loss of the soul; eternal damnation
29.	PERNICIOUS	Deadly; destructive; wicked
30.	PITEOUS	Demanding or arousing pity
31.	PORTENTOUS	Full of unspecifiable significance; exciting wonder and awe
32.	PRODIGAL	Rashly or wastefully extravagant
33.	REPLICATION	A reply to an answer; a rejoinder
34.	SCOURGE	A means of inflicting severe suffering, vengeance or punishment
35.	SINEWS	Tendon; muscles
36.	SUPERFLUOUS	Being beyond what is required or sufficient
37.	VISAGE	The face or facial expression
38.	VOW	An earnest promise

Hamlet Vocabulary Fill In The Blanks 1

_____ 1. Immune to attack; impregnable; impossible to damage, injure, or wound

_____ 2. A reply to an answer; a rejoinder

_____ 3. To address an earnest or urgent request to

_____ 4. High praise

_____ 5. Influence or effect by a supernatural power

_____ 6. Difficult to work with

_____ 7. To make an earnest request of

_____ 8. A harmful, corrupting influence

_____ 9. To plan with cleverness or ingenuity; scheme

_____ 10. Becoming known

_____ 11. Mixed together

_____ 12. Spiteful

_____ 13. Loss of the soul; eternal damnation

_____ 14. The relationship of child or offspring to parent

_____ 15. To inflict grievous physical or mental suffering on

_____ 16. Assembly

_____ 17. An inscription on a tombstone in memory of the one buried there

_____ 18. Rashly or wastefully extravagant

_____ 19. Ability or power to decide responsibly

_____ 20. Open to more than one interpretation

Hamlet Vocabulary Fill In The Blanks 1 Answer Key

INVULNERABLE	1. Immune to attack; impregnable; impossible to damage, injure, or wound
REPLICATION	2. A reply to an answer; a rejoinder
BESEECH	3. To address an earnest or urgent request to
EXTOLMENT	4. High praise
CONJURATION	5. Influence or effect by a supernatural power
CHURLISH	6. Difficult to work with
ENTREAT	7. To make an earnest request of
CONTAGION	8. A harmful, corrupting influence
CONTRIVE	9. To plan with cleverness or ingenuity; scheme
DIVULGING	10. Becoming known
COMMINGLED	11. Mixed together
MALICIOUS	12. Spiteful
PERDITION	13. Loss of the soul; eternal damnation
FILIAL	14. The relationship of child or offspring to parent
AFFLICT	15. To inflict grievous physical or mental suffering on
CONVOCATION	16. Assembly
EPITAPH	17. An inscription on a tombstone in memory of the one buried there
PRODIGAL	18. Rashly or wastefully extravagant
DISCRETION	19. Ability or power to decide responsibly
AMBIGUOUS	20. Open to more than one interpretation

Hamlet Vocabulary Fill In The Blanks 2

1. Reduction in amount, degree, or intensity
2. Difficult to work with
3. An inscription on a tombstone in memory of the one buried there
4. To address an earnest or urgent request to
5. Of or relating to the body or flesh; bodily
6. Tension or strife
7. Great happiness; bliss
8. A reply to an answer; a rejoinder
9. Something added to another, more important thing; an appendage
10. A model of excellence or perfection
11. Full of unspecifiable significance; exciting wonder and awe
12. Becoming known
13. To plan with cleverness or ingenuity; scheme
14. Distant physically or emotionally
15. Ability or power to decide responsibly
16. Mixed together
17. About to occur; impending
18. Demanding or arousing pity
19. Tendon; muscles
20. To inflict grievous physical or mental suffering on

Hamlet Vocabulary Fill In The Blanks 2 Answer Key

ABATEMENTS	1. Reduction in amount, degree, or intensity
CHURLISH	2. Difficult to work with
EPITAPH	3. An inscription on a tombstone in memory of the one buried there
BESEECH	4. To address an earnest or urgent request to
CARNAL	5. Of or relating to the body or flesh; bodily
DISCORD	6. Tension or strife
FELICITY	7. Great happiness; bliss
REPLICATION	8. A reply to an answer; a rejoinder
APPURTENANCE	9. Something added to another, more important thing; an appendage
PARAGON	10. A model of excellence or perfection
PORTENTOUS	11. Full of unspecifiable significance; exciting wonder and awe
DIVULGING	12. Becoming known
CONTRIVE	13. To plan with cleverness or ingenuity; scheme
ALOOF	14. Distant physically or emotionally
DISCRETION	15. Ability or power to decide responsibly
COMMINGLED	16. Mixed together
IMMINENT	17. About to occur; impending
PITEOUS	18. Demanding or arousing pity
SINEWS	19. Tendon; muscles
AFFLICT	20. To inflict grievous physical or mental suffering on

Hamlet Vocabulary Fill In The Blanks 3

1. Tendon; muscles
2. The relationship of child or offspring to parent
3. Deadly; destructive; wicked
4. The lowest or bottom part
5. Something added to another, more important thing; an appendage
6. Rashly or wastefully extravagant
7. Loss of the soul; eternal damnation
8. Of or relating to the body or flesh; bodily
9. Spiteful
10. Assembly
11. To address an earnest or urgent request to
12. High praise
13. A harmful, corrupting influence
14. Unprincipled
15. Reduction in amount, degree, or intensity
16. Difficult to work with
17. The face or facial expression
18. An inscription on a tombstone in memory of the one buried there
19. Mixed together
20. A means of inflicting severe suffering, vengeance or punishment

Hamlet Vocabulary Fill In The Blanks 3 Answer Key

SINEWS	1. Tendon; muscles
FILIAL	2. The relationship of child or offspring to parent
PERNICIOUS	3. Deadly; destructive; wicked
BASE	4. The lowest or bottom part
APPURTENANCE	5. Something added to another, more important thing; an appendage
PRODIGAL	6. Rashly or wastefully extravagant
PERDITION	7. Loss of the soul; eternal damnation
CARNAL	8. Of or relating to the body or flesh; bodily
MALICIOUS	9. Spiteful
CONVOCATION	10. Assembly
BESEECH	11. To address an earnest or urgent request to
EXTOLMENT	12. High praise
CONTAGION	13. A harmful, corrupting influence
KNAVISH	14. Unprincipled
ABATEMENTS	15. Reduction in amount, degree, or intensity
CHURLISH	16. Difficult to work with
VISAGE	17. The face or facial expression
EPITAPH	18. An inscription on a tombstone in memory of the one buried there
COMMINGLED	19. Mixed together
SCOURGE	20. A means of inflicting severe suffering, vengeance or punishment

Hamlet Vocabulary Fill In The Blanks 4

_____ 1. To plan with cleverness or ingenuity; scheme

_____ 2. Ability or power to decide responsibly

_____ 3. A means of inflicting severe suffering, vengeance or punishment

_____ 4. A harmful, corrupting influence

_____ 5. To address an earnest or urgent request to

_____ 6. Open to more than one interpretation

_____ 7. A model of excellence or perfection

_____ 8. About to occur; impending

_____ 9. The face or facial expression

_____ 10. Tension or strife

_____ 11. Reduction in amount, degree, or intensity

_____ 12. Loss of the soul; eternal damnation

_____ 13. Full of unspecifiable significance; exciting wonder and awe

_____ 14. Immune to attack; impregnable; impossible to damage, injure, or wound

_____ 15. Difficult to work with

_____ 16. Something added to another, more important thing; an appendage

_____ 17. Rashly or wastefully extravagant

_____ 18. Assembly

_____ 19. To make an earnest request of

_____ 20. The relationship of child or offspring to parent

Hamlet Vocabulary Fill In The Blanks 4 Answer Key

CONTRIVE	1. To plan with cleverness or ingenuity; scheme
DISCRETION	2. Ability or power to decide responsibly
SCOURGE	3. A means of inflicting severe suffering, vengeance or punishment
CONTAGION	4. A harmful, corrupting influence
BESEECH	5. To address an earnest or urgent request to
AMBIGUOUS	6. Open to more than one interpretation
PARAGON	7. A model of excellence or perfection
IMMINENT	8. About to occur; impending
VISAGE	9. The face or facial expression
DISCORD	10. Tension or strife
ABATEMENTS	11. Reduction in amount, degree, or intensity
PERDITION	12. Loss of the soul; eternal damnation
PORTENTOUS	13. Full of unspecifiable significance; exciting wonder and awe
INVULNERABLE	14. Immune to attack; impregnable; impossible to damage, injure, or wound
CHURLISH	15. Difficult to work with
APPURTENANCE	16. Something added to another, more important thing; an appendage
PRODIGAL	17. Rashly or wastefully extravagant
CONVOCATION	18. Assembly
ENTREAT	19. To make an earnest request of
FILIAL	20. The relationship of child or offspring to parent

Hamlet Vocabulary Matching 1

___ 1. AMBIGUOUS   A. An inscription on a tombstone in memory of the one buried there
___ 2. PARAGON   B. Unprincipled
___ 3. INVULNERABLE   C. Loss of the soul; eternal damnation
___ 4. COMMINGLED   D. Immune to attack; impregnable; impossible to damage, injure, or wound
___ 5. EPITAPH   E. The relationship of child or offspring to parent
___ 6. AFFLICT   F. Being beyond what is required or sufficient
___ 7. PERNICIOUS   G. An earnest promise
___ 8. EXTOLMENT   H. Mixed together
___ 9. CONTAGION   I. Open to more than one interpretation
___ 10. DISCRETION   J. Tendon; muscles
___ 11. BESEECH   K. Of or relating to the body or flesh; bodily
___ 12. SINEWS   L. High praise
___ 13. APPURTENANCE   M. A harmful, corrupting influence
___ 14. CONTRIVE   N. Reduction in amount, degree, or intensity
___ 15. PERDITION   O. A model of excellence or perfection
___ 16. REPLICATION   P. Something added to another, more important thing; an appendage
___ 17. ABATEMENTS   Q. Tension or strife
___ 18. CARNAL   R. Deadly; destructive; wicked
___ 19. DISCORD   S. To plan with cleverness or ingenuity; scheme
___ 20. PRODIGAL   T. Difficult to work with
___ 21. VOW   U. To address an earnest or urgent request to
___ 22. FILIAL   V. A reply to an answer; a rejoinder
___ 23. SUPERFLUOUS   W. Ability or power to decide responsibly
___ 24. CHURLISH   X. To inflict grievous physical or mental suffering on
___ 25. KNAVISH   Y. Rashly or wastefully extravagant

Hamlet Vocabulary Matching 1 Answer Key

I - 1. AMBIGUOUS	A. An inscription on a tombstone in memory of the one buried there
O - 2. PARAGON	B. Unprincipled
D - 3. INVULNERABLE	C. Loss of the soul; eternal damnation
H - 4. COMMINGLED	D. Immune to attack; impregnable; impossible to damage, injure, or wound
A - 5. EPITAPH	E. The relationship of child or offspring to parent
X - 6. AFFLICT	F. Being beyond what is required or sufficient
R - 7. PERNICIOUS	G. An earnest promise
L - 8. EXTOLMENT	H. Mixed together
M - 9. CONTAGION	I. Open to more than one interpretation
W - 10. DISCRETION	J. Tendon; muscles
U - 11. BESEECH	K. Of or relating to the body or flesh; bodily
J - 12. SINEWS	L. High praise
P - 13. APPURTENANCE	M. A harmful, corrupting influence
S - 14. CONTRIVE	N. Reduction in amount, degree, or intensity
C - 15. PERDITION	O. A model of excellence or perfection
V - 16. REPLICATION	P. Something added to another, more important thing; an appendage
N - 17. ABATEMENTS	Q. Tension or strife
K - 18. CARNAL	R. Deadly; destructive; wicked
Q - 19. DISCORD	S. To plan with cleverness or ingenuity; scheme
Y - 20. PRODIGAL	T. Difficult to work with
G - 21. VOW	U. To address an earnest or urgent request to
E - 22. FILIAL	V. A reply to an answer; a rejoinder
F - 23. SUPERFLUOUS	W. Ability or power to decide responsibly
T - 24. CHURLISH	X. To inflict grievous physical or mental suffering on
B - 25. KNAVISH	Y. Rashly or wastefully extravagant

Hamlet Vocabulary Matching 2

___ 1. EPITAPH   A. Influence or effect by a supernatural power
___ 2. BASE   B. Being beyond what is required or sufficient
___ 3. PRODIGAL   C. Deadly; destructive; wicked
___ 4. PORTENTOUS   D. Tendon; muscles
___ 5. KNAVISH   E. A reply to an answer; a rejoinder
___ 6. ENTREAT   F. High praise
___ 7. CHURLISH   G. Difficult to work with
___ 8. DISCORD   H. To make an earnest request of
___ 9. PERNICIOUS   I. To address an earnest or urgent request to
___10. ABATEMENTS   J. Full of unspecifiable significance; exciting wonder and awe
___11. CARNAL   K. A model of excellence or perfection
___12. BESEECH   L. Tension or strife
___13. PERDITION   M. Reduction in amount, degree, or intensity
___14. DISCRETION   N. An inscription on a tombstone in memory of the one buried there
___15. EXTOLMENT   O. Mixed together
___16. IMMINENT   P. To inflict grievous physical or mental suffering on
___17. PARAGON   Q. Of or relating to the body or flesh; bodily
___18. AFFLICT   R. Rashly or wastefully extravagant
___19. REPLICATION   S. To plan with cleverness or ingenuity; scheme
___20. CONJURATION   T. About to occur; impending
___21. CONVOCATION   U. Unprincipled
___22. CONTRIVE   V. The lowest or bottom part
___23. COMMINGLED   W. Loss of the soul; eternal damnation
___24. SUPERFLUOUS   X. Assembly
___25. SINEWS   Y. Ability or power to decide responsibly

Hamlet Vocabulary Matching 2 Answer Key

N - 1.	EPITAPH	A. Influence or effect by a supernatural power
V - 2.	BASE	B. Being beyond what is required or sufficient
R - 3.	PRODIGAL	C. Deadly; destructive; wicked
J - 4.	PORTENTOUS	D. Tendon; muscles
U - 5.	KNAVISH	E. A reply to an answer; a rejoinder
H - 6.	ENTREAT	F. High praise
G - 7.	CHURLISH	G. Difficult to work with
L - 8.	DISCORD	H. To make an earnest request of
C - 9.	PERNICIOUS	I. To address an earnest or urgent request to
M -10.	ABATEMENTS	J. Full of unspecifiable significance; exciting wonder and awe
Q -11.	CARNAL	K. A model of excellence or perfection
I -12.	BESEECH	L. Tension or strife
W -13.	PERDITION	M. Reduction in amount, degree, or intensity
Y -14.	DISCRETION	N. An inscription on a tombstone in memory of the one buried there
F -15.	EXTOLMENT	O. Mixed together
T -16.	IMMINENT	P. To inflict grievous physical or mental suffering on
K -17.	PARAGON	Q. Of or relating to the body or flesh; bodily
P -18.	AFFLICT	R. Rashly or wastefully extravagant
E -19.	REPLICATION	S. To plan with cleverness or ingenuity; scheme
A -20.	CONJURATION	T. About to occur; impending
X -21.	CONVOCATION	U. Unprincipled
S -22.	CONTRIVE	V. The lowest or bottom part
O -23.	COMMINGLED	W. Loss of the soul; eternal damnation
B -24.	SUPERFLUOUS	X. Assembly
D -25.	SINEWS	Y. Ability or power to decide responsibly

Hamlet Vocabulary Matching 3

___ 1. DIVULGING
___ 2. CONTAGION
___ 3. REPLICATION
___ 4. INVULNERABLE
___ 5. CHURLISH
___ 6. CONTRIVE
___ 7. SCOURGE
___ 8. DISCORD
___ 9. PERDITION
___ 10. PERNICIOUS
___ 11. COMMINGLED
___ 12. SUPERFLUOUS
___ 13. AFFLICT
___ 14. DISCRETION
___ 15. CARNAL
___ 16. VOW
___ 17. PITEOUS
___ 18. BESEECH
___ 19. APPURTENANCE
___ 20. CONVOCATION
___ 21. ENTREAT
___ 22. MALICIOUS
___ 23. IMMINENT
___ 24. ALOOF
___ 25. FELICITY

A. A means of inflicting severe suffering, vengeance or punishment
B. Great happiness; bliss
C. Mixed together
D. Immune to attack; impregnable; impossible to damage, injure, or wound
E. Spiteful
F. Deadly; destructive; wicked
G. Becoming known
H. Tension or strife
I. A harmful, corrupting influence
J. A reply to an answer; a rejoinder
K. About to occur; impending
L. Demanding or arousing pity
M. To plan with cleverness or ingenuity; scheme
N. To make an earnest request of
O. Something added to another, more important thing; an appendage
P. Of or relating to the body or flesh; bodily
Q. To address an earnest or urgent request to
R. An earnest promise
S. Difficult to work with
T. To inflict grievous physical or mental suffering on
U. Ability or power to decide responsibly
V. Loss of the soul; eternal damnation
W. Distant physically or emotionally
X. Assembly
Y. Being beyond what is required or sufficient

Hamlet Vocabulary Matching 3 Answer Key

G - 1. DIVULGING	A.	A means of inflicting severe suffering, vengeance or punishment
I - 2. CONTAGION	B.	Great happiness; bliss
J - 3. REPLICATION	C.	Mixed together
D - 4. INVULNERABLE	D.	Immune to attack; impregnable; impossible to damage, injure, or wound
S - 5. CHURLISH	E.	Spiteful
M - 6. CONTRIVE	F.	Deadly; destructive; wicked
A - 7. SCOURGE	G.	Becoming known
H - 8. DISCORD	H.	Tension or strife
V - 9. PERDITION	I.	A harmful, corrupting influence
F - 10. PERNICIOUS	J.	A reply to an answer; a rejoinder
C - 11. COMMINGLED	K.	About to occur; impending
Y - 12. SUPERFLUOUS	L.	Demanding or arousing pity
T - 13. AFFLICT	M.	To plan with cleverness or ingenuity; scheme
U - 14. DISCRETION	N.	To make an earnest request of
P - 15. CARNAL	O.	Something added to another, more important thing; an appendage
R - 16. VOW	P.	Of or relating to the body or flesh; bodily
L - 17. PITEOUS	Q.	To address an earnest or urgent request to
Q - 18. BESEECH	R.	An earnest promise
O - 19. APPURTENANCE	S.	Difficult to work with
X - 20. CONVOCATION	T.	To inflict grievous physical or mental suffering on
N - 21. ENTREAT	U.	Ability or power to decide responsibly
E - 22. MALICIOUS	V.	Loss of the soul; eternal damnation
K - 23. IMMINENT	W.	Distant physically or emotionally
W - 24. ALOOF	X.	Assembly
B - 25. FELICITY	Y.	Being beyond what is required or sufficient

Hamlet Vocabulary Matching 4

___ 1. FELICITY
___ 2. COMMINGLED
___ 3. PITEOUS
___ 4. BASE
___ 5. VOW
___ 6. ENTREAT
___ 7. ALOOF
___ 8. CONTRIVE
___ 9. PORTENTOUS
___ 10. FILIAL
___ 11. EXTOLMENT
___ 12. IMMINENT
___ 13. REPLICATION
___ 14. SCOURGE
___ 15. PRODIGAL
___ 16. DISCORD
___ 17. INVULNERABLE
___ 18. APPURTENANCE
___ 19. AFFLICT
___ 20. CARNAL
___ 21. SINEWS
___ 22. CONTAGION
___ 23. EPITAPH
___ 24. SUPERFLUOUS
___ 25. AMBIGUOUS

A. High praise
B. The lowest or bottom part
C. Demanding or arousing pity
D. To plan with cleverness or ingenuity; scheme
E. The relationship of child or offspring to parent
F. Tendon; muscles
G. Open to more than one interpretation
H. Of or relating to the body or flesh; bodily
I. Tension or strife
J. A reply to an answer; a rejoinder
K. Full of unspecifiable significance; exciting wonder and awe
L. Rashly or wastefully extravagant
M. About to occur; impending
N. Something added to another, more important thing; an appendage
O. Immune to attack; impregnable; impossible to damage, injure, or wound
P. A harmful, corrupting influence
Q. Great happiness; bliss
R. Mixed together
S. To make an earnest request of
T. Being beyond what is required or sufficient
U. Distant physically or emotionally
V. An earnest promise
W. A means of inflicting severe suffering, vengeance or punishment
X. To inflict grievous physical or mental suffering on
Y. An inscription on a tombstone in memory of the one buried there

Hamlet Vocabulary Matching 4 Answer Key

Q - 1. FELICITY		A. High praise
R - 2. COMMINGLED		B. The lowest or bottom part
C - 3. PITEOUS		C. Demanding or arousing pity
B - 4. BASE		D. To plan with cleverness or ingenuity; scheme
V - 5. VOW		E. The relationship of child or offspring to parent
S - 6. ENTREAT		F. Tendon; muscles
U - 7. ALOOF		G. Open to more than one interpretation
D - 8. CONTRIVE		H. Of or relating to the body or flesh; bodily
K - 9. PORTENTOUS		I. Tension or strife
E - 10. FILIAL		J. A reply to an answer; a rejoinder
A - 11. EXTOLMENT		K. Full of unspecifiable significance; exciting wonder and awe
M - 12. IMMINENT		L. Rashly or wastefully extravagant
J - 13. REPLICATION		M. About to occur; impending
W - 14. SCOURGE		N. Something added to another, more important thing; an appendage
L - 15. PRODIGAL		O. Immune to attack; impregnable; impossible to damage, injure, or wound
I - 16. DISCORD		P. A harmful, corrupting influence
O - 17. INVULNERABLE		Q. Great happiness; bliss
N - 18. APPURTENANCE		R. Mixed together
X - 19. AFFLICT		S. To make an earnest request of
H - 20. CARNAL		T. Being beyond what is required or sufficient
F - 21. SINEWS		U. Distant physically or emotionally
P - 22. CONTAGION		V. An earnest promise
Y - 23. EPITAPH		W. A means of inflicting severe suffering, vengeance or punishment
T - 24. SUPERFLUOUS		X. To inflict grievous physical or mental suffering on
G - 25. AMBIGUOUS		Y. An inscription on a tombstone in memory of the one buried there

Hamlet Vocabulary Magic Squares 1

Match the definition with the vocabulary word. Put your answers in the magic squares below. When your answers are correct, all columns and rows will add to the same number.

A. INVULNERABLE
B. DIVULGING
C. BASE
D. KNAVISH
E. IMMINENT
F. PERNICIOUS
G. CARNAL
H. DISCORD
I. VOW
J. CONJURATION
K. CONTAGION
L. EPITAPH
M. PRODIGAL
N. SCOURGE
O. VISAGE
P. ALOOF

1. Tension or strife
2. Rashly or wastefully extravagant
3. Becoming known
4. A harmful, corrupting influence
5. Influence or effect by a supernatural power
6. The lowest or bottom part
7. Distant physically or emotionally
8. About to occur; impending
9. The face or facial expression
10. Deadly; destructive; wicked
11. An earnest promise
12. Unprincipled
13. Immune to attack; impregnable; impossible to damage, injure, or wound
14. An inscription on a tombstone in memory of the one buried there
15. Of or relating to the body or flesh; bodily
16. A means of inflicting severe suffering, vengeance or punishment

A=	B=	C=	D=
E=	F=	G=	H=
I=	J=	K=	L=
M=	N=	O=	P=

Hamlet Vocabulary Magic Squares 1 Answer Key

Match the definition with the vocabulary word. Put your answers in the magic squares below. When your answers are correct, all columns and rows will add to the same number.

A. INVULNERABLE
B. DIVULGING
C. BASE
D. KNAVISH
E. IMMINENT
F. PERNICIOUS
G. CARNAL
H. DISCORD
I. VOW
J. CONJURATION
K. CONTAGION
L. EPITAPH
M. PRODIGAL
N. SCOURGE
O. VISAGE
P. ALOOF

1. Tension or strife
2. Rashly or wastefully extravagant
3. Becoming known
4. A harmful, corrupting influence
5. Influence or effect by a supernatural power
6. The lowest or bottom part
7. Distant physically or emotionally
8. About to occur; impending
9. The face or facial expression
10. Deadly; destructive; wicked
11. An earnest promise
12. Unprincipled
13. Immune to attack; impregnable; impossible to damage, injure, or wound
14. An inscription on a tombstone in memory of the one buried there
15. Of or relating to the body or flesh; bodily
16. A means of inflicting severe suffering, vengeance or punishment

A=13	B=3	C=6	D=12
E=8	F=10	G=15	H=1
I=11	J=5	K=4	L=14
M=2	N=16	O=9	P=7

Hamlet Vocabulary Magic Squares 2

Match the definition with the vocabulary word. Put your answers in the magic squares below. When your answers are correct, all columns and rows will add to the same number.

A. PARAGON
B. CONTRIVE
C. AMBIGUOUS
D. IMMINENT
E. ENTREAT
F. EPITAPH
G. SCOURGE
H. MALICIOUS
I. FELICITY
J. SINEWS
K. DISCRETION
L. KNAVISH
M. PITEOUS
N. DIVULGING
O. SUPERFLUOUS
P. BESEECH

1. A model of excellence or perfection
2. Becoming known
3. Tendon; muscles
4. To make an earnest request of
5. A means of inflicting severe suffering, vengeance or punishment
6. Unprincipled
7. To address an earnest or urgent request to
8. Open to more than one interpretation
9. Being beyond what is required or sufficient
10. About to occur; impending
11. Spiteful
12. Ability or power to decide responsibly
13. Great happiness; bliss
14. An inscription on a tombstone in memory of the one buried there
15. To plan with cleverness or ingenuity; scheme
16. Demanding or arousing pity

A=	B=	C=	D=
E=	F=	G=	H=
I=	J=	K=	L=
M=	N=	O=	P=

Hamlet Vocabulary Magic Squares 2 Answer Key

Match the definition with the vocabulary word. Put your answers in the magic squares below. When your answers are correct, all columns and rows will add to the same number.

A. PARAGON
B. CONTRIVE
C. AMBIGUOUS
D. IMMINENT
E. ENTREAT
F. EPITAPH
G. SCOURGE
H. MALICIOUS
I. FELICITY
J. SINEWS
K. DISCRETION
L. KNAVISH
M. PITEOUS
N. DIVULGING
O. SUPERFLUOUS
P. BESEECH

1. A model of excellence or perfection
2. Becoming known
3. Tendon; muscles
4. To make an earnest request of
5. A means of inflicting severe suffering, vengeance or punishment
6. Unprincipled
7. To address an earnest or urgent request to
8. Open to more than one interpretation
9. Being beyond what is required or sufficient
10. About to occur; impending
11. Spiteful
12. Ability or power to decide responsibly
13. Great happiness; bliss
14. An inscription on a tombstone in memory of the one buried there
15. To plan with cleverness or ingenuity; scheme
16. Demanding or arousing pity

A=1	B=15	C=8	D=10
E=4	F=14	G=5	H=11
I=13	J=3	K=12	L=6
M=16	N=2	O=9	P=7

Hamlet Vocabulary Magic Squares 3

Match the definition with the vocabulary word. Put your answers in the magic squares below. When your answers are correct, all columns and rows will add to the same number.

A. KNAVISH
B. PITEOUS
C. CONJURATION
D. FELICITY
E. PERDITION
F. CARNAL
G. VISAGE
H. DISCRETION
I. EXTOLMENT
J. DIVULGING
K. SINEWS
L. IMMINENT
M. BASE
N. CONTAGION
O. SUPERFLUOUS
P. CONTRIVE

1. Being beyond what is required or sufficient
2. Great happiness; bliss
3. Becoming known
4. Loss of the soul; eternal damnation
5. High praise
6. Of or relating to the body or flesh; bodily
7. To plan with cleverness or ingenuity; scheme
8. Influence or effect by a supernatural power
9. Ability or power to decide responsibly
10. Tendon; muscles
11. Unprincipled
12. A harmful, corrupting influence
13. Demanding or arousing pity
14. The lowest or bottom part
15. The face or facial expression
16. About to occur; impending

A=	B=	C=	D=
E=	F=	G=	H=
I=	J=	K=	L=
M=	N=	O=	P=

Hamlet Vocabulary Magic Squares 3 Answer Key

Match the definition with the vocabulary word. Put your answers in the magic squares below. When your answers are correct, all columns and rows will add to the same number.

A. KNAVISH
B. PITEOUS
C. CONJURATION
D. FELICITY
E. PERDITION
F. CARNAL
G. VISAGE
H. DISCRETION
I. EXTOLMENT
J. DIVULGING
K. SINEWS
L. IMMINENT
M. BASE
N. CONTAGION
O. SUPERFLUOUS
P. CONTRIVE

1. Being beyond what is required or sufficient
2. Great happiness; bliss
3. Becoming known
4. Loss of the soul; eternal damnation
5. High praise
6. Of or relating to the body or flesh; bodily
7. To plan with cleverness or ingenuity; scheme
8. Influence or effect by a supernatural power
9. Ability or power to decide responsibly
10. Tendon; muscles
11. Unprincipled
12. A harmful, corrupting influence
13. Demanding or arousing pity
14. The lowest or bottom part
15. The face or facial expression
16. About to occur; impending

A=11	B=13	C=8	D=2
E=4	F=6	G=15	H=9
I=5	J=3	K=10	L=16
M=14	N=12	O=1	P=7

Hamlet Vocabulary Magic Squares 4

Match the definition with the vocabulary word. Put your answers in the magic squares below. When your answers are correct, all columns and rows will add to the same number.

A. MALICIOUS
B. AMBIGUOUS
C. FELICITY
D. PERNICIOUS
E. CONTRIVE
F. AFFLICT
G. PITEOUS
H. FILIAL
I. INVULNERABLE
J. VISAGE
K. COMMINGLED
L. DIVULGING
M. PERDITION
N. CONTAGION
O. IMMINENT
P. EPITAPH

1. Loss of the soul; eternal damnation
2. To inflict grievous physical or mental suffering on
3. The relationship of child or offspring to parent
4. About to occur; impending
5. Becoming known
6. Great happiness; bliss
7. Spiteful
8. The face or facial expression
9. Mixed together
10. Deadly; destructive; wicked
11. Open to more than one interpretation
12. Immune to attack; impregnable; impossible to damage, injure, or wound
13. A harmful, corrupting influence
14. To plan with cleverness or ingenuity; scheme
15. Demanding or arousing pity
16. An inscription on a tombstone in memory of the one buried there

A=	B=	C=	D=
E=	F=	G=	H=
I=	J=	K=	L=
M=	N=	O=	P=

Hamlet Vocabulary Magic Squares 4 Answer Key

Match the definition with the vocabulary word. Put your answers in the magic squares below. When your answers are correct, all columns and rows will add to the same number.

A. MALICIOUS
B. AMBIGUOUS
C. FELICITY
D. PERNICIOUS
E. CONTRIVE
F. AFFLICT
G. PITEOUS
H. FILIAL
I. INVULNERABLE
J. VISAGE
K. COMMINGLED
L. DIVULGING
M. PERDITION
N. CONTAGION
O. IMMINENT
P. EPITAPH

1. Loss of the soul; eternal damnation
2. To inflict grievous physical or mental suffering on
3. The relationship of child or offspring to parent
4. About to occur; impending
5. Becoming known
6. Great happiness; bliss
7. Spiteful
8. The face or facial expression
9. Mixed together
10. Deadly; destructive; wicked
11. Open to more than one interpretation
12. Immune to attack; impregnable; impossible to damage, injure, or wound
13. A harmful, corrupting influence
14. To plan with cleverness or ingenuity; scheme
15. Demanding or arousing pity
16. An inscription on a tombstone in memory of the one buried there

A=7	B=11	C=6	D=10
E=14	F=2	G=15	H=3
I=12	J=8	K=9	L=5
M=1	N=13	O=4	P=16

Hamlet Vocabulary Word Search 1

```
D G A S F R E P L I C A T I O N Y E D Q
I C F U I B B I F E R Z W N T Y L W I D
V O F P L S V T D P Z R X L B B N L S X
U N L E I T N E N I M M I K A Y A T C Z
L J I R A N D O J T Z F J R C G W K R Y
G U C F L E C U R A P D E H I Q Q H E Q
I R T L W M F S Z P D N M D M D S A T X
N A N U M E T M N H L X O M D I Y M I H
G T Y O P T S K T U W R N Q L X Y B O V
F I D U Y A P X V P P W Q R V B P I N Q
Y O F S C B L N S E P V U N J X E G X J
K N H L G A I U F R P H C L X X R U E Z
Z N Q Y J S O P F D C H T J T C N O N X
N C A G F I Y X E I B D W O Q O I U T L
L O H V C H Q H L T E F L V C N C S R J
L N H I I C J P I I S M T I Q T I V E K
J T L P Z S Y X C O E M B S P R O O A F
C A R N A L S H S I N E W S A J I U W T R
M G L Q W P Q R T P C L R G S V S R B T
J I X O M Y D N Y D H A S E W E T T P Y
K O T P O Z M Q F G G D I S C O R D C J
T N X X C F X Z C O M M I N G L E D F N
N O I T A C O V N O C S C O U R G E M C
```

A harmful, corrupting influence (9)
A means of inflicting severe suffering, vengeance or punishment (7)
A model of excellence or perfection (7)
A reply to an answer; a rejoinder (11)
Ability or power to decide responsibly (10)
About to occur; impending (8)
An earnest promise (3)
An inscription on a tombstone in memory of the one buried there (7)
Assembly (11)
Becoming known (9)
Being beyond what is required or sufficient (11)
Deadly; destructive; wicked (10)
Demanding or arousing pity (7)
Difficult to work with (8)
Distant physically or emotionally (5)
Great happiness; bliss (8)
High praise (9)
Immune to attack; impregnable; impossible to damage, injure, or wound (12)
Influence or effect by a supernatural power (11)
Loss of the soul; eternal damnation (9)
Mixed together (10)
Of or relating to the body or flesh; bodily (6)
Open to more than one interpretation (9)
Rashly or wastefully extravagant (8)
Reduction in amount, degree, or intensity (10)
Spiteful (9)
Tendon; muscles (6)
Tension or strife (7)
The face or facial expression (6)
The lowest or bottom part (4)
The relationship of child or offspring to parent (6)
To address an earnest or urgent request to (7)
To inflict grievous physical or mental suffering on (7)
To make an earnest request of (7)
To plan with cleverness or ingenuity; scheme (8)
Unprincipled (7)

Hamlet Vocabulary Word Search 1 Answer Key

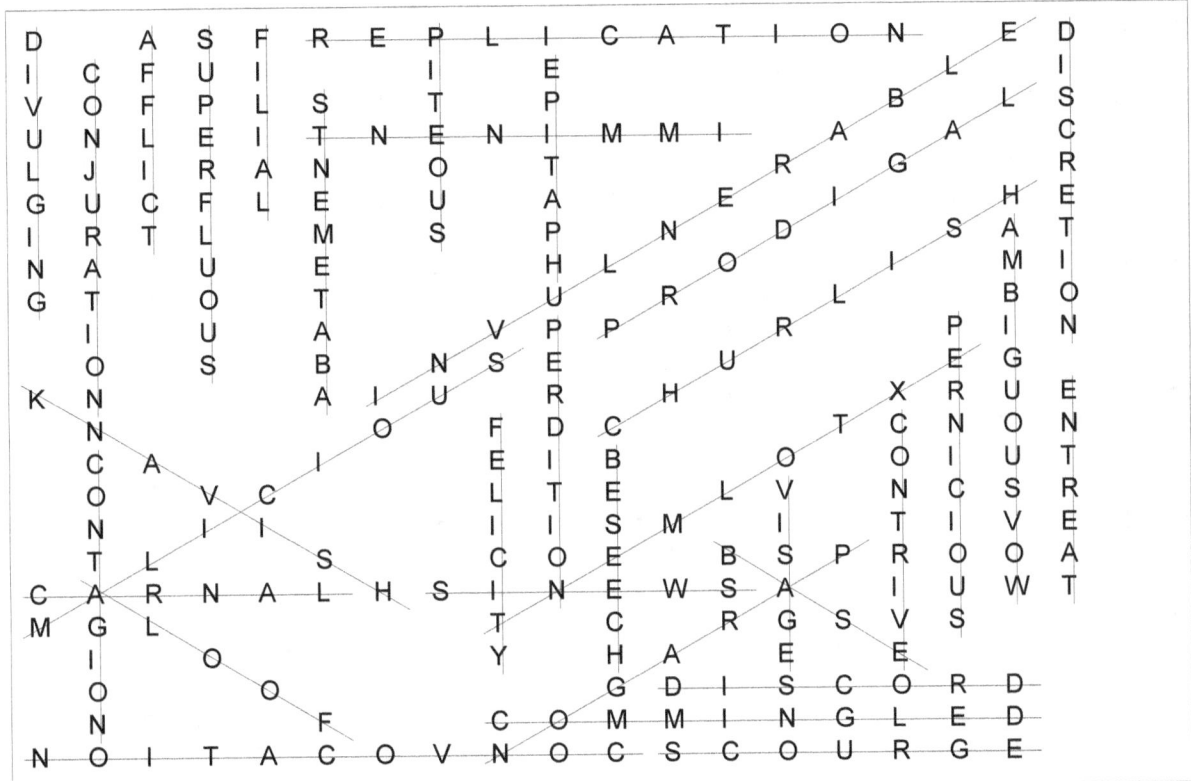

A harmful, corrupting influence (9)
A means of inflicting severe suffering, vengeance or punishment (7)
A model of excellence or perfection (7)
A reply to an answer; a rejoinder (11)
Ability or power to decide responsibly (10)
About to occur; impending (8)
An earnest promise (3)
An inscription on a tombstone in memory of the one buried there (7)
Assembly (11)
Becoming known (9)
Being beyond what is required or sufficient (11)
Deadly; destructive; wicked (10)
Demanding or arousing pity (7)
Difficult to work with (8)
Distant physically or emotionally (5)
Great happiness; bliss (8)
High praise (9)
Immune to attack; impregnable; impossible to damage, injure, or wound (12)
Influence or effect by a supernatural power (11)
Loss of the soul; eternal damnation (9)
Mixed together (10)
Of or relating to the body or flesh; bodily (6)
Open to more than one interpretation (9)
Rashly or wastefully extravagant (8)
Reduction in amount, degree, or intensity (10)
Spiteful (9)
Tendon; muscles (6)
Tension or strife (7)
The face or facial expression (6)
The lowest or bottom part (4)
The relationship of child or offspring to parent (6)
To address an earnest or urgent request to (7)
To inflict grievous physical or mental suffering on (7)
To make an earnest request of (7)
To plan with cleverness or ingenuity; scheme (8)
Unprincipled (7)

Hamlet Vocabulary Word Search 2

```
C M E D I S C R E T I O N G Z H S Y T K
R W X Z Y A R Y T G D E L G N I M M O C
M K T Z L N F M A L I C I O U S T P B H
P Z O L J S I F H P C N N M Y S G V S R
Y V L R L S M F L V C A W J C G T I S Q
C C M C W L M Q V I W N W O Q J V H J Y
V O E E G T I Z K B C E N Z Y A E W K Z
R X N R C N J U R A T I O N F L R H Y
C I T T C B E C P R R M K O G B P D Q
S Z B P A F N J L I K U K M I B A F I T
P P H A A G T R V O W P R E T T R E S Y
E I O X S R I E L N Y P G A I C E L C V
R F T R C E A O M Q N A E P D A N I O Z
N I A E T S G N K S R E L R R L C R P
I L L T O E Y N O I T C A L E N U I D K
C I O Y B U N V V N C G O Y P A V T S S
I A O R E M S T E C I F D U H L N Y G R
O L F N S D Q C O D L C H U R L I S H R
U T Y R E G Q S O U D B L Z D G V Y F B
S N H H E F J R M Y S M Q Z G K E Z S B
G W K W C Y P Z S D I V U L G I N G T Z
W T J R H C O N V O C A T I O N G M B S
R E P L I C A T I O N A M B I G U O U S
```

A harmful, corrupting influence (9)
A means of inflicting severe suffering, vengeance or punishment (7)
A model of excellence or perfection (7)
A reply to an answer; a rejoinder (11)
Ability or power to decide responsibly (10)
About to occur; impending (8)
An earnest promise (3)
An inscription on a tombstone in memory of the one buried there (7)
Assembly (11)
Becoming known (9)
Deadly; destructive; wicked (10)
Demanding or arousing pity (7)
Difficult to work with (8)
Distant physically or emotionally (5)
Full of unspecifiable significance; exciting wonder and awe (10)
Great happiness; bliss (8)
High praise (9)
Immune to attack; impregnable; impossible to damage, injure, or wound (12)
Influence or effect by a supernatural power (11)
Loss of the soul; eternal damnation (9)
Mixed together (10)
Of or relating to the body or flesh; bodily (6)
Open to more than one interpretation (9)
Rashly or wastefully extravagant (8)
Something added to another, more important thing; an appendage (12)
Spiteful (9)
Tendon; muscles (6)
Tension or strife (7)
The face or facial expression (6)
The lowest or bottom part (4)
The relationship of child or offspring to parent (6)
To address an earnest or urgent request to (7)
To inflict grievous physical or mental suffering on (7)
To make an earnest request of (7)
To plan with cleverness or ingenuity; scheme (8)
Unprincipled (7)

Hamlet Vocabulary Word Search 2 Answer Key

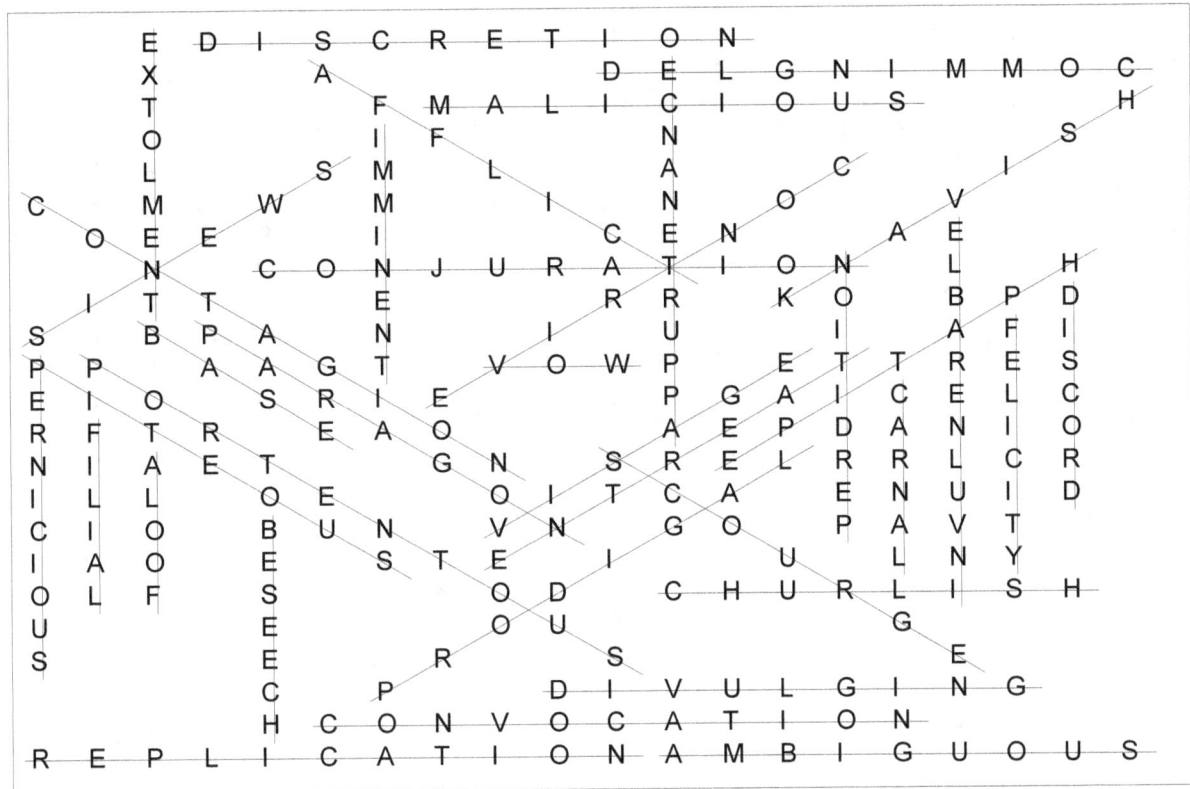

- A harmful, corrupting influence (9)
- A means of inflicting severe suffering, vengeance or punishment (7)
- A model of excellence or perfection (7)
- A reply to an answer; a rejoinder (11)
- Ability or power to decide responsibly (10)
- About to occur; impending (8)
- An earnest promise (3)
- An inscription on a tombstone in memory of the one buried there (7)
- Assembly (11)
- Becoming known (9)
- Deadly; destructive; wicked (10)
- Demanding or arousing pity (7)
- Difficult to work with (8)
- Distant physically or emotionally (5)
- Full of unspecifiable significance; exciting wonder and awe (10)
- Great happiness; bliss (8)
- High praise (9)
- Immune to attack; impregnable; impossible to damage, injure, or wound (12)
- Influence or effect by a supernatural power (11)
- Loss of the soul; eternal damnation (9)
- Mixed together (10)
- Of or relating to the body or flesh; bodily (6)
- Open to more than one interpretation (9)
- Rashly or wastefully extravagant (8)
- Something added to another, more important thing; an appendage (12)
- Spiteful (9)
- Tendon; muscles (6)
- Tension or strife (7)
- The face or facial expression (6)
- The lowest or bottom part (4)
- The relationship of child or offspring to parent (6)
- To address an earnest or urgent request to (7)
- To inflict grievous physical or mental suffering on (7)
- To make an earnest request of (7)
- To plan with cleverness or ingenuity; scheme (8)
- Unprincipled (7)

Hamlet Vocabulary Word Search 3

```
I N V U L N E R A B L E P I T E O U S S R
C O C D P P F C S T N E M E T N J B A S Q
Z I O I E T J D W N H Q F R N J P Q S U S
C T N V R C N D E R N Z S P O R O Y P N
N E V U N V F X N O J U H E I K R W E V
X R O L I F Y D I N O B Y R T A T C R K
N C C G C R W T S U T C T D A F F V F X
P S A I I X A B G F J B C I C F N I L V
D I T N O R Z I Y I Q W Y T I L T S U Q
M D I G U G B T N L G W V I L I O A O J
H P O J S M I N M I Z L M O P C U G U H
L A N R A C C P T A E R T N E T S E S G
Q O Z L I O O K R L L R T S R C L I I B
C J O L B M N N H O N I A B O L V E M K
D O E B W M M D T H D B C U L A H X M V
F F V O W I R I Q A V I R I N C C T I F
K L E Y D N I S Q S G G G K O H E O N P
J L P Y G G V C X H E I G A X U E L E S
T X I V Q L E O W B Q H O R L R S M N R
W G T B H E D R L S K G R N M L E E T L
Y L A Y J D K D X P V S Z P M I B N J K
A P P U R T E N A N C E Q C T S Y T M F
B Y H P A R A G O N T R M T Y H T P T H
```

ABATEMENTS	CONVOCATION	PARAGON
AFFLICT	DISCORD	PERDITION
ALOOF	DISCRETION	PERNICIOUS
AMBIGUOUS	DIVULGING	PITEOUS
APPURTENANCE	ENTREAT	PORTENTOUS
BASE	EPITAPH	PRODIGAL
BESEECH	EXTOLMENT	REPLICATION
CARNAL	FELICITY	SCOURGE
CHURLISH	FILIAL	SINEWS
COMMINGLED	IMMINENT	SUPERFLUOUS
CONJURATION	INVULNERABLE	VISAGE
CONTAGION	KNAVISH	VOW
CONTRIVE	MALICIOUS	

Hamlet Vocabulary Word Search 3 Answer Key

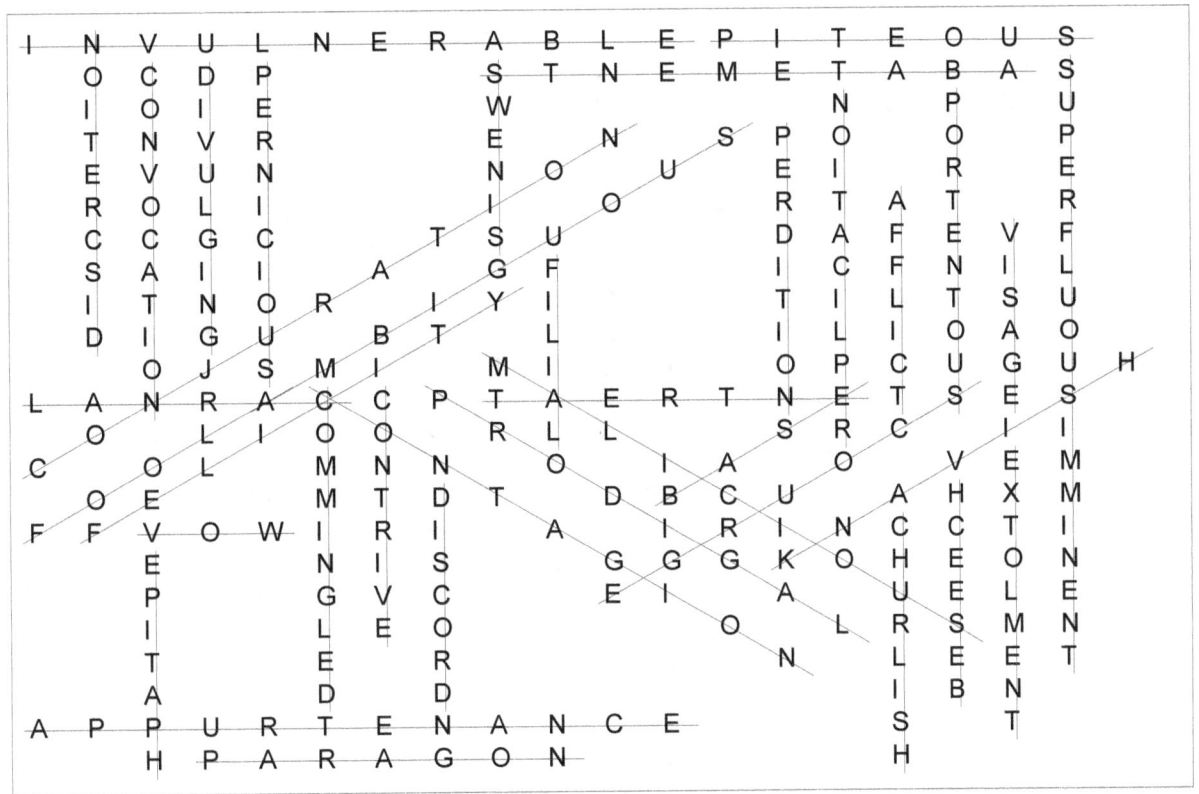

ABATEMENTS	CONVOCATION	PARAGON
AFFLICT	DISCORD	PERDITION
ALOOF	DISCRETION	PERNICIOUS
AMBIGUOUS	DIVULGING	PITEOUS
APPURTENANCE	ENTREAT	PORTENTOUS
BASE	EPITAPH	PRODIGAL
BESEECH	EXTOLMENT	REPLICATION
CARNAL	FELICITY	SCOURGE
CHURLISH	FILIAL	SINEWS
COMMINGLED	IMMINENT	SUPERFLUOUS
CONJURATION	INVULNERABLE	VISAGE
CONTAGION	KNAVISH	VOW
CONTRIVE	MALICIOUS	

Hamlet Vocabulary Word Search 4

```
C M C Q Q M P V V F S Y W Z Z B L Q F E
O A O V K Q E D I I U R I D C N G R G H
N L N O L S R P S L O D O Z T M R Q X
T I V W A S D H A I I A M B I G U O U S
A C O B G T I Q G A C M I W H O F G A Y
G I C X I Q T D E L I T N W C J Q O J M
I O A X D P I P T N N T E S H S U P J P
O U T N O B D G S R K N P P L P B A F
N S I D R H N L C I E V T O F U F R E L
B T O V P L E K Z N P F R R R B A L P F
B N N J N D Z J Y E C W E T N G I T I C
C E S U O E T I P W D P E E O C Z C A G
H M S Y I J K E J S U N L N I G R I P G
U E R E T R V B W S A B G T T N V L H L
R T K E I J T Z N A Z Y O A R M F X Y
L A W X R C T V C R B V D U C F E F X D
I B J T C T H E E Q L R X S I A W A D R
S A N O S S F N X H O K B W L F R G T K
H O G L I C L Y A C T P V H P K P N M C
C X K M D U V D S L F F S G E G W L X L
K V N E V B Q I S G O F K T R H S T L
L Q G N B D D K D J W O B T R J N B G Z
N O I T A R U J N O C T F K N A V I S H
```

ABATEMENTS   CONVOCATION   PERDITION

AFFLICT   DISCORD   PERNICIOUS

ALOOF   DISCRETION   PITEOUS

AMBIGUOUS   ENTREAT   PORTENTOUS

APPURTENANCE   EPITAPH   PRODIGAL

BASE   EXTOLMENT   REPLICATION

BESEECH   FELICITY   SCOURGE

CARNAL   FILIAL   SINEWS

CHURLISH   IMMINENT   SUPERFLUOUS

COMMINGLED   INVULNERABLE   VISAGE

CONJURATION   KNAVISH   VOW

CONTAGION   MALICIOUS

CONTRIVE   PARAGON

Hamlet Vocabulary Word Search 4 Answer Key

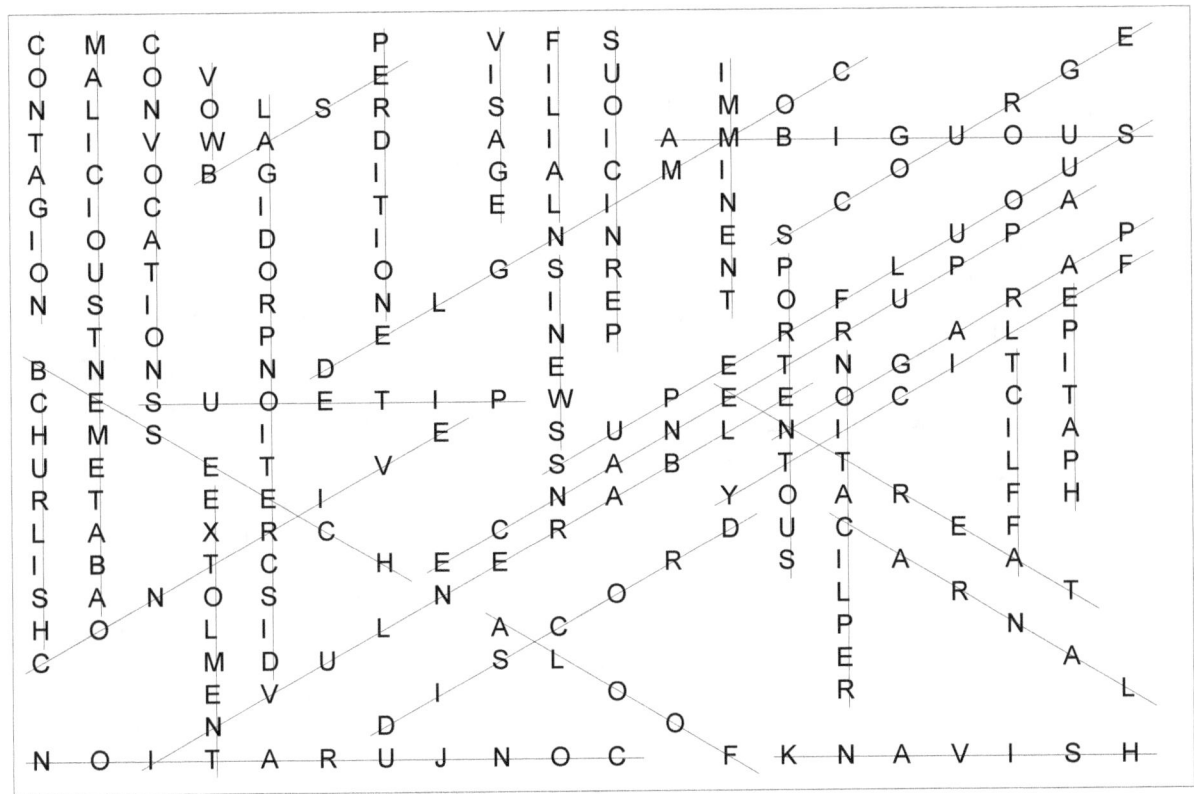

ABATEMENTS	CONVOCATION	PERDITION
AFFLICT	DISCORD	PERNICIOUS
ALOOF	DISCRETION	PITEOUS
AMBIGUOUS	ENTREAT	PORTENTOUS
APPURTENANCE	EPITAPH	PRODIGAL
BASE	EXTOLMENT	REPLICATION
BESEECH	FELICITY	SCOURGE
CARNAL	FILIAL	SINEWS
CHURLISH	IMMINENT	SUPERFLUOUS
COMMINGLED	INVULNERABLE	VISAGE
CONJURATION	KNAVISH	VOW
CONTAGION	MALICIOUS	
CONTRIVE	PARAGON	

Hamlet Vocabulary Crossword 1

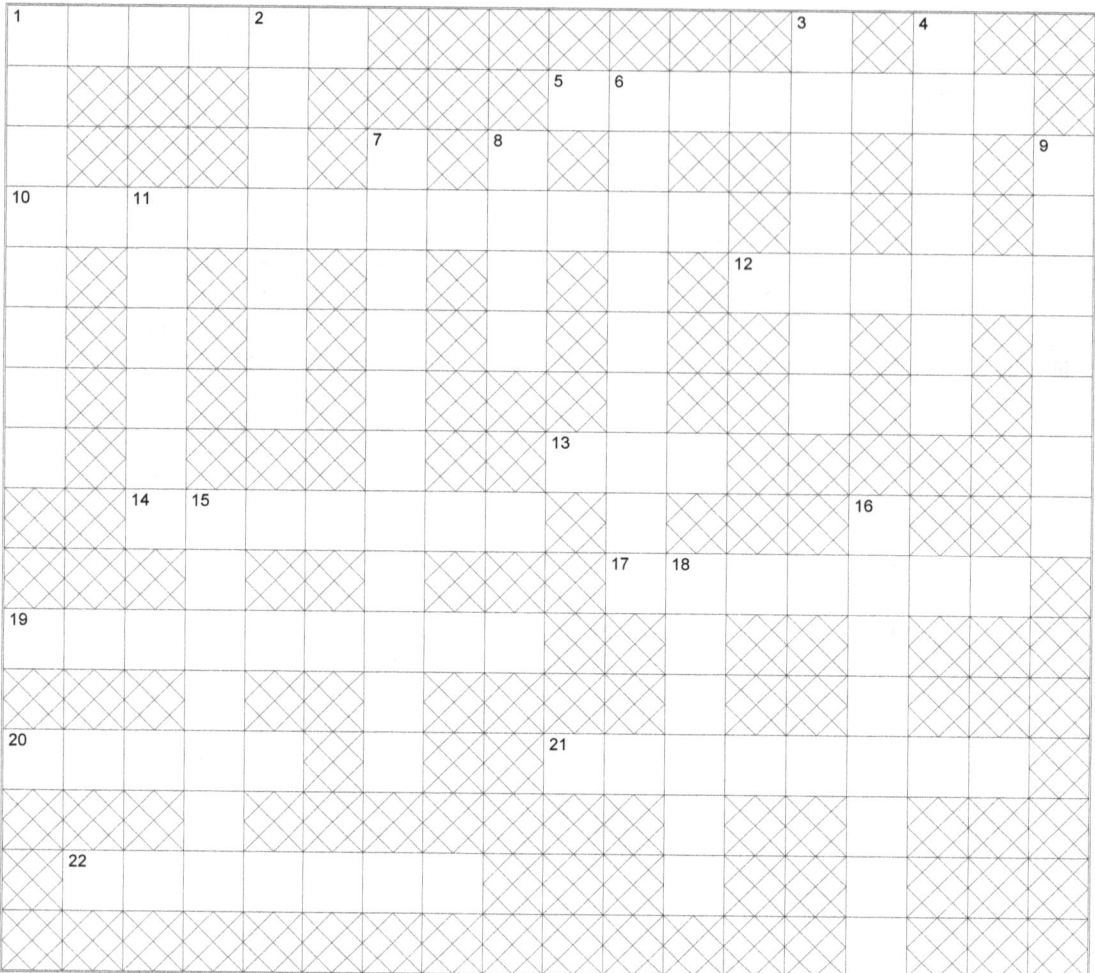

Across
1. The relationship of child or offspring to parent
5. About to occur; impending
10. Immune to attack; impregnable; impossible to damage, injure, or wound
12. Tendon; muscles
13. An earnest promise
14. An inscription on a tombstone in memory of the one buried there
17. A means of inflicting severe suffering, vengeance or punishment
19. A harmful, corrupting influence
20. Distant physically or emotionally
21. To plan with cleverness or ingenuity; scheme
22. Tension or strife

Down
1. Great happiness; bliss
2. To inflict grievous physical or mental suffering on
3. Unprincipled
4. To make an earnest request of
6. Spiteful
7. A reply to an answer; a rejoinder
8. The lowest or bottom part
9. To address an earnest or urgent request to
11. The face or facial expression
15. Demanding or arousing pity
16. Rashly or wastefully extravagant
18. Of or relating to the body or flesh; bodily

Hamlet Vocabulary Crossword 1 Answer Key

	1 F	I	L	I	2 A	L						3 K		4 E	
	E				F				5 I	6 M	M	I	N	E	N	T
	L				F		7 R		8 B		A		N		T		9 B
10 I	N	11 V	U	L	N	E	R	A	B	L	E		A	12 S	I	N	E	W	S
	C		I		I		P		S		I			S		A		E
	I		S		C		L		E		C			H		T		E
	T		A		T		I				I		13 V	O	W			C
	Y		G				C									16 P		H
		14 E	15 P	I	T	A	P	H		U				
			I				T		17 S	18 C	O	U	R	G	E
19 C	O	N	T	A	G	I	O	N		A		O		
			E				O			R		D		
20 A	L	O	O	F		N			21 C	O	N	T	R	I	V	E
			U							A		G		
		22 D	I	S	C	O	R	D		L		A		
												L		

Across
1. The relationship of child or offspring to parent
5. About to occur; impending
10. Immune to attack; impregnable; impossible to damage, injure, or wound
12. Tendon; muscles
13. An earnest promise
14. An inscription on a tombstone in memory of the one buried there
17. A means of inflicting severe suffering, vengeance or punishment
19. A harmful, corrupting influence
20. Distant physically or emotionally
21. To plan with cleverness or ingenuity; scheme
22. Tension or strife

Down
1. Great happiness; bliss
2. To inflict grievous physical or mental suffering on
3. Unprincipled
4. To make an earnest request of
6. Spiteful
7. A reply to an answer; a rejoinder
8. The lowest or bottom part
9. To address an earnest or urgent request to
11. The face or facial expression
15. Demanding or arousing pity
16. Rashly or wastefully extravagant
18. Of or relating to the body or flesh; bodily

Hamlet Vocabulary Crossword 2

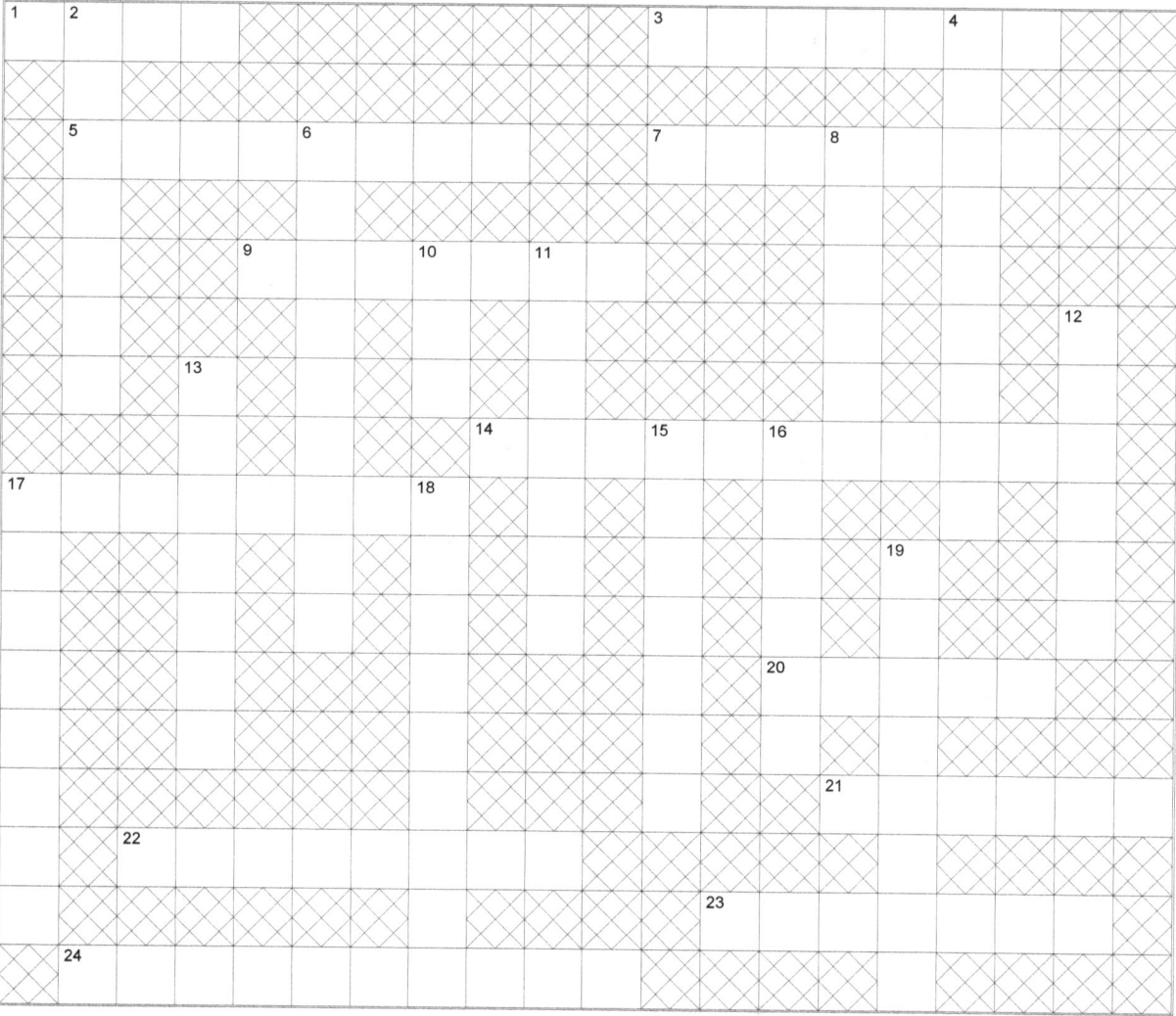

Across
1. The lowest or bottom part
3. An inscription on a tombstone in memory of the one buried there
5. Great happiness; bliss
7. Tension or strife
9. Unprincipled
14. Being beyond what is required or sufficient
17. To plan with cleverness or ingenuity; scheme
20. Distant physically or emotionally
21. Tendon; muscles
22. About to occur; impending
23. A model of excellence or perfection
24. Full of unspecifiable significance; exciting wonder and awe

Down
2. To inflict grievous physical or mental suffering on
4. Loss of the soul; eternal damnation
6. A harmful, corrupting influence
8. Of or relating to the body or flesh; bodily
10. An earnest promise
11. A means of inflicting severe suffering, vengeance or punishment
12. The face or facial expression
13. Demanding or arousing pity
15. To make an earnest request of
16. The relationship of child or offspring to parent
17. Difficult to work with
18. High praise
19. Rashly or wastefully extravagant

Hamlet Vocabulary Crossword 2 Answer Key

	1 B	2 A	S	E				3 E	P	I	T	A	4 P	H	
		F											E		
		5 F	E	L	I	6 C	I	T	Y		7 D	I	8 C	O	R	D
		L				O							A		D	
		I			9 K	N	A	10 V	I	11 S	H		R		I	
		C				T		O		C			N		T	12 V
		T		13 P	A	G	W		O			A		I	I
				I			G		14 S	U	P	15 E	R	16 F	L	U	O	U	S
17 C	O	N	T	R	I	V	18 E		R			N		I			N		A
H				E			O		X			G		T		L		19 P		G
U				O			N		T			E		R		I		R		E
R				U					O					E		20 A	L	O	O	F
L				S					L					A		L		D		
I									M					T		21 S	I	N	E	W	S
S		22 I	M	M	I	N	E	N	T							G				
H							N							23 P	A	R	A	G	O	N
		24 P	O	R	T	E	N	T	O	U	S					L				

Across
1. The lowest or bottom part
3. An inscription on a tombstone in memory of the one buried there
5. Great happiness; bliss
7. Tension or strife
9. Unprincipled
14. Being beyond what is required or sufficient
17. To plan with cleverness or ingenuity; scheme
20. Distant physically or emotionally
21. Tendon; muscles
22. About to occur; impending
23. A model of excellence or perfection
24. Full of unspecifiable significance; exciting wonder and awe

Down
2. To inflict grievous physical or mental suffering on
4. Loss of the soul; eternal damnation
6. A harmful, corrupting influence
8. Of or relating to the body or flesh; bodily
10. An earnest promise
11. A means of inflicting severe suffering, vengeance or punishment
12. The face or facial expression
13. Demanding or arousing pity
15. To make an earnest request of
16. The relationship of child or offspring to parent
17. Difficult to work with
18. High praise
19. Rashly or wastefully extravagant

Hamlet Vocabulary Crossword 3

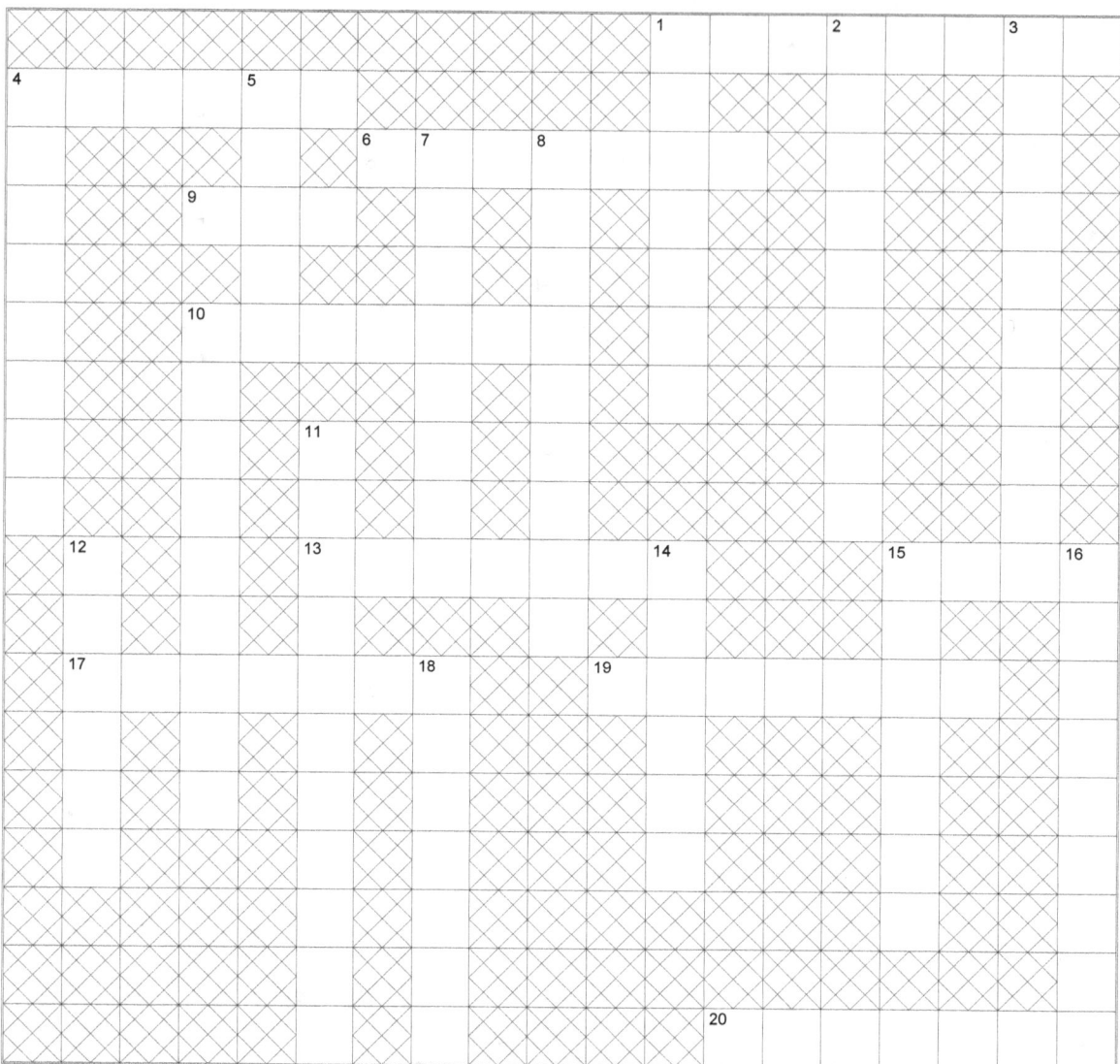

Across
1. Rashly or wastefully extravagant
4. The relationship of child or offspring to parent
6. Tension or strife
9. An earnest promise
10. To inflict grievous physical or mental suffering on
13. Demanding or arousing pity
15. The lowest or bottom part
17. A means of inflicting severe suffering, vengeance or punishment
19. Unprincipled
20. To make an earnest request of

Down
1. A model of excellence or perfection
2. Becoming known
3. Reduction in amount, degree, or intensity
4. Great happiness; bliss
5. Distant physically or emotionally
7. About to occur; impending
8. A harmful, corrupting influence
10. Open to more than one interpretation
11. Being beyond what is required or sufficient
12. The face or facial expression
14. Tendon; muscles
15. To address an earnest or urgent request to
16. High praise
18. An inscription on a tombstone in memory of the one buried there

Hamlet Vocabulary Crossword 3 Answer Key

Across
1. Rashly or wastefully extravagant
4. The relationship of child or offspring to parent
6. Tension or strife
9. An earnest promise
10. To inflict grievous physical or mental suffering on
13. Demanding or arousing pity
15. The lowest or bottom part
17. A means of inflicting severe suffering, vengeance or punishment
19. Unprincipled
20. To make an earnest request of

Down
1. A model of excellence or perfection
2. Becoming known
3. Reduction in amount, degree, or intensity
4. Great happiness; bliss
5. Distant physically or emotionally
7. About to occur; impending
8. A harmful, corrupting influence
10. Open to more than one interpretation
11. Being beyond what is required or sufficient
12. The face or facial expression
14. Tendon; muscles
15. To address an earnest or urgent request to
16. High praise
18. An inscription on a tombstone in memory of the one buried there

Hamlet Vocabulary Crossword 4

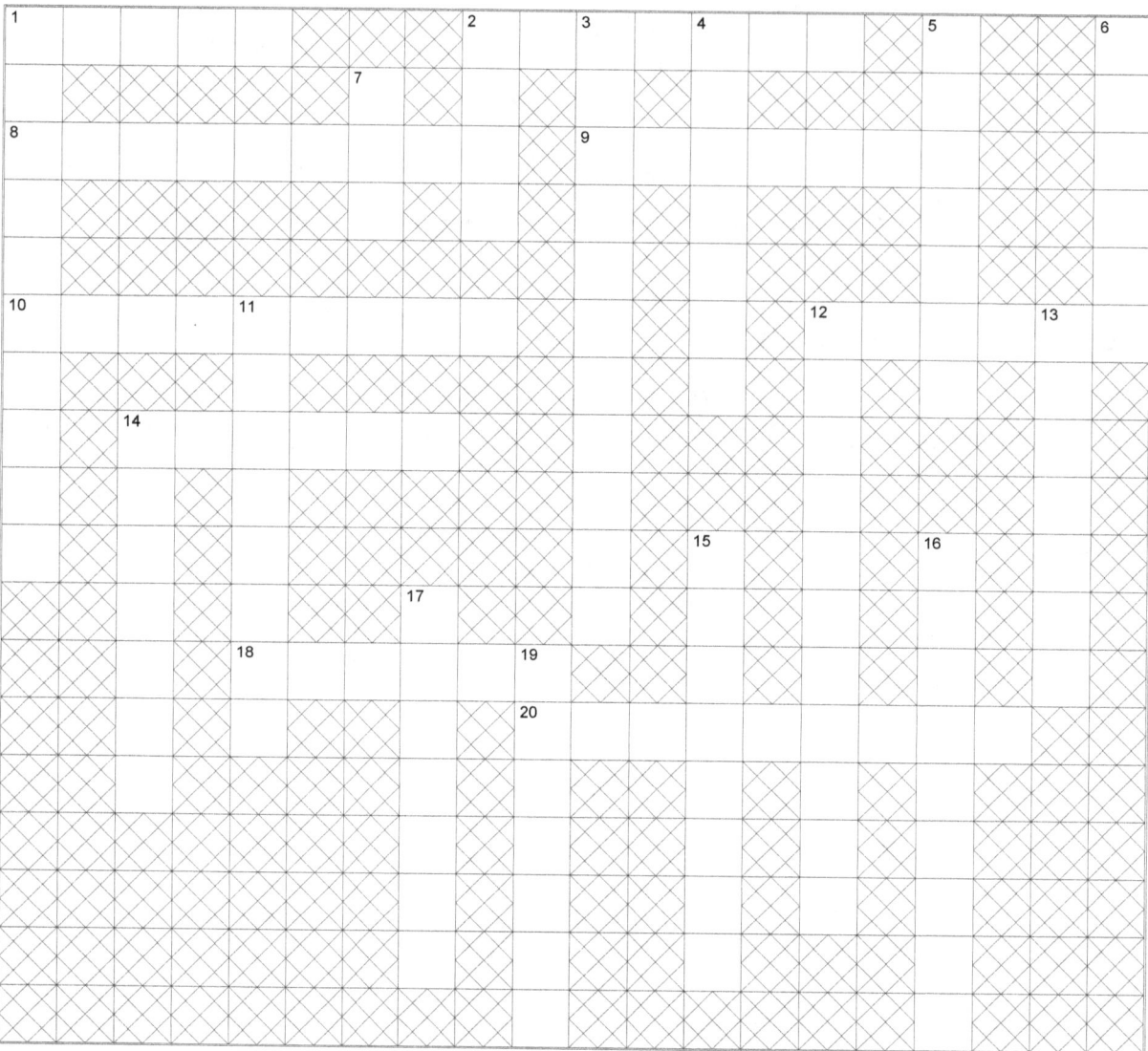

Across
1. Distant physically or emotionally
2. To address an earnest or urgent request to
8. Open to more than one interpretation
9. Demanding or arousing pity
10. Spiteful
12. Of or relating to the body or flesh; bodily
14. Tendon; muscles
18. The face or facial expression
20. Loss of the soul; eternal damnation

Down
1. Reduction in amount, degree, or intensity
2. The lowest or bottom part
3. Being beyond what is required or sufficient
4. To make an earnest request of
5. Tension or strife
6. The relationship of child or offspring to parent
7. An earnest promise
11. To plan with cleverness or ingenuity; scheme
12. Assembly
13. To inflict grievous physical or mental suffering on
14. A means of inflicting severe suffering, vengeance or punishment
15. Rashly or wastefully extravagant
16. High praise
17. A model of excellence or perfection
19. An inscription on a tombstone in memory of the one buried there

Hamlet Vocabulary Crossword 4 Answer Key

Across
1. Distant physically or emotionally
2. To address an earnest or urgent request to
8. Open to more than one interpretation
9. Demanding or arousing pity
10. Spiteful
12. Of or relating to the body or flesh; bodily
14. Tendon; muscles
18. The face or facial expression
20. Loss of the soul; eternal damnation

Down
1. Reduction in amount, degree, or intensity
2. The lowest or bottom part
3. Being beyond what is required or sufficient
4. To make an earnest request of
5. Tension or strife
6. The relationship of child or offspring to parent
7. An earnest promise
11. To plan with cleverness or ingenuity; scheme
12. Assembly
13. To inflict grievous physical or mental suffering on
14. A means of inflicting severe suffering, vengeance or punishment
15. Rashly or wastefully extravagant
16. High praise
17. A model of excellence or perfection
19. An inscription on a tombstone in memory of the one buried there

Hamlet Vocabulary Juggle Letters 1

1. RLHIHUSC = 1. _____
   Difficult to work with

2. NRTECIVO = 2. _____
   To plan with cleverness or ingenuity; scheme

3. TCROIEDNIS = 3. _____
   Ability or power to decide responsibly

4. SCIRODD = 4. _____
   Tension or strife

5. OUBAMUSIG = 5. _____
   Open to more than one interpretation

6. IPHEAPT = 6. _____
   An inscription on a tombstone in memory of the one buried there

7. IIUGVNLGD = 7. _____
   Becoming known

8. SNKIHAV = 8. _____
   Unprincipled

9. OVIAONTCNCO = 9. _____
   Assembly

10. STAEATNMEB =10. _____
    Reduction in amount, degree, or intensity

11. REDNOTIIP =11. _____
    Loss of the soul; eternal damnation

12. IAOSCMLIU =12. _____
    Spiteful

13. SVIAEG =13. _____
    The face or facial expression

14. FCFAILT =14. _____
    To inflict grievous physical or mental suffering on

15. UOSSULURFPE =15. _____
    Being beyond what is required or sufficient

Hamlet Vocabulary Juggle Letters 1 Answer Key

1. RLHIHUSC = 1. CHURLISH
   Difficult to work with

2. NRTECIVO = 2. CONTRIVE
   To plan with cleverness or ingenuity; scheme

3. TCROIEDNIS = 3. DISCRETION
   Ability or power to decide responsibly

4. SCIRODD = 4. DISCORD
   Tension or strife

5. OUBAMUSIG = 5. AMBIGUOUS
   Open to more than one interpretation

6. IPHEAPT = 6. EPITAPH
   An inscription on a tombstone in memory of the one buried there

7. IIUGVNLGD = 7. DIVULGING
   Becoming known

8. SNKIHAV = 8. KNAVISH
   Unprincipled

9. OVIAONTCNCO = 9. CONVOCATION
   Assembly

10. STAEATNMEB =10. ABATEMENTS
    Reduction in amount, degree, or intensity

11. REDNOTIIP =11. PERDITION
    Loss of the soul; eternal damnation

12. IAOSCMLIU =12. MALICIOUS
    Spiteful

13. SVIAEG =13. VISAGE
    The face or facial expression

14. FCFAILT =14. AFFLICT
    To inflict grievous physical or mental suffering on

15. UOSSULURFPE =15. SUPERFLUOUS
    Being beyond what is required or sufficient

Hamlet Vocabulary Juggle Letters 2

1. OANAGPR = 1. _____
   A model of excellence or perfection

2. HBEECSE = 2. _____
   To address an earnest or urgent request to

3. NCOONTOICVA = 3. _____
   Assembly

4. FSRUUOSLUEP = 4. _____
   Being beyond what is required or sufficient

5. SULIRHCH = 5. _____
   Difficult to work with

6. MINMCGLEDO = 6. _____
   Mixed together

7. ACNALR = 7. _____
   Of or relating to the body or flesh; bodily

8. FAOLO = 8. _____
   Distant physically or emotionally

9. BTSAMANEET = 9. _____
   Reduction in amount, degree, or intensity

10. REANTET =10. _____
    To make an earnest request of

11. NROSTPOTUE =11. _____
    Full of unspecifiable significance; exciting wonder and awe

12. FILTCFA =12. _____
    To inflict grievous physical or mental suffering on

13. TDPEONIIR =13. _____
    Loss of the soul; eternal damnation

14. ATLERIPNICO =14. _____
    A reply to an answer; a rejoinder

15. ILIAFL =15. _____
    The relationship of child or offspring to parent

Hamlet Vocabulary Juggle Letters 2 Answer Key

1. OANAGPR = 1. PARAGON
   A model of excellence or perfection

2. HBEECSE = 2. BESEECH
   To address an earnest or urgent request to

3. NCOONTOICVA = 3. CONVOCATION
   Assembly

4. FSRUUOSLUEP = 4. SUPERFLUOUS
   Being beyond what is required or sufficient

5. SULIRHCH = 5. CHURLISH
   Difficult to work with

6. MINMCGLEDO = 6. COMMINGLED
   Mixed together

7. ACNALR = 7. CARNAL
   Of or relating to the body or flesh; bodily

8. FAOLO = 8. ALOOF
   Distant physically or emotionally

9. BTSAMANEET = 9. ABATEMENTS
   Reduction in amount, degree, or intensity

10. REANTET =10. ENTREAT
    To make an earnest request of

11. NROSTPOTUE =11. PORTENTOUS
    Full of unspecifiable significance; exciting wonder and awe

12. FILTCFA =12. AFFLICT
    To inflict grievous physical or mental suffering on

13. TDPEONIIR =13. PERDITION
    Loss of the soul; eternal damnation

14. ATLERIPNICO =14. REPLICATION
    A reply to an answer; a rejoinder

15. ILIAFL =15. FILIAL
    The relationship of child or offspring to parent

Hamlet Vocabulary Juggle Letters 3

1. ANEETSMTAB = 1. _____
   Reduction in amount, degree, or intensity

2. VKIHSNA = 2. _____
   Unprincipled

3. ESUNIRCOPI = 3. _____
   Deadly; destructive; wicked

4. GDILMECNOM = 4. _____
   Mixed together

5. ENSSWI = 5. _____
   Tendon; muscles

6. MTXOLTNEE = 6. _____
   High praise

7. GLIPDAOR = 7. _____
   Rashly or wastefully extravagant

8. LANIVNBEULER = 8. _____
   Immune to attack; impregnable; impossible to damage, injure, or wound

9. RIDOCSD = 9. _____
   Tension or strife

10. NPORGAA = 10. _____
    A model of excellence or perfection

11. TERONVIC = 11. _____
    To plan with cleverness or ingenuity; scheme

12. OLAFO = 12. _____
    Distant physically or emotionally

13. EUSTIOP = 13. _____
    Demanding or arousing pity

14. NLICATEIPOR = 14. _____
    A reply to an answer; a rejoinder

15. TNEATRE = 15. _____
    To make an earnest request of

Hamlet Vocabulary Juggle Letters 3 Answer Key

1. ANEETSMTAB = 1. ABATEMENTS
   Reduction in amount, degree, or intensity

2. VKIHSNA = 2. KNAVISH
   Unprincipled

3. ESUNIRCOPI = 3. PERNICIOUS
   Deadly; destructive; wicked

4. GDILMECNOM = 4. COMMINGLED
   Mixed together

5. ENSSWI = 5. SINEWS
   Tendon; muscles

6. MTXOLTNEE = 6. EXTOLMENT
   High praise

7. GLIPDAOR = 7. PRODIGAL
   Rashly or wastefully extravagant

8. LANIVNBEULER = 8. INVULNERABLE
   Immune to attack; impregnable; impossible to damage, injure, or wound

9. RIDOCSD = 9. DISCORD
   Tension or strife

10. NPORGAA = 10. PARAGON
    A model of excellence or perfection

11. TERONVIC = 11. CONTRIVE
    To plan with cleverness or ingenuity; scheme

12. OLAFO = 12. ALOOF
    Distant physically or emotionally

13. EUSTIOP = 13. PITEOUS
    Demanding or arousing pity

14. NLICATEIPOR = 14. REPLICATION
    A reply to an answer; a rejoinder

15. TNEATRE = 15. ENTREAT
    To make an earnest request of

Hamlet Vocabulary Juggle Letters 4

1. NTICRILAOEP = 1. _____
   A reply to an answer; a rejoinder

2. CFIELTYI = 2. _____
   Great happiness; bliss

3. MINTMNIE = 3. _____
   About to occur; impending

4. GNAOAPR = 4. _____
   A model of excellence or perfection

5. ANCRAL = 5. _____
   Of or relating to the body or flesh; bodily

6. TLFIACF = 6. _____
   To inflict grievous physical or mental suffering on

7. SEAB = 7. _____
   The lowest or bottom part

8. BAEAESTMTN = 8. _____
   Reduction in amount, degree, or intensity

9. OIPSUENICR = 9. _____
   Deadly; destructive; wicked

10. ITPUOES = 10. _____
    Demanding or arousing pity

11. LRSESUPFUOU = 11. _____
    Being beyond what is required or sufficient

12. EATTERN = 12. _____
    To make an earnest request of

13. MGNECMLIOD = 13. _____
    Mixed together

14. ODENIRTIP = 14. _____
    Loss of the soul; eternal damnation

15. OCOCIVAONNT = 15. _____
    Assembly

Hamlet Vocabulary Juggle Letters 4 Answer Key

1. NTICRILAOEP = 1. REPLICATION
   A reply to an answer; a rejoinder

2. CFIELTYI = 2. FELICITY
   Great happiness; bliss

3. MINTMNIE = 3. IMMINENT
   About to occur; impending

4. GNAOAPR = 4. PARAGON
   A model of excellence or perfection

5. ANCRAL = 5. CARNAL
   Of or relating to the body or flesh; bodily

6. TLFIACF = 6. AFFLICT
   To inflict grievous physical or mental suffering on

7. SEAB = 7. BASE
   The lowest or bottom part

8. BAEAESTMTN = 8. ABATEMENTS
   Reduction in amount, degree, or intensity

9. OIPSUENICR = 9. PERNICIOUS
   Deadly; destructive; wicked

10. ITPUOES =10. PITEOUS
    Demanding or arousing pity

11. LRSESUPFUOU =11. SUPERFLUOUS
    Being beyond what is required or sufficient

12. EATTERN =12. ENTREAT
    To make an earnest request of

13. MGNECMLIOD =13. COMMINGLED
    Mixed together

14. ODENIRTIP =14. PERDITION
    Loss of the soul; eternal damnation

15. OCOCIVAONNT =15. CONVOCATION
    Assembly

ABATEMENTS	Reduction in amount, degree, or intensity
AFFLICT	To inflict grievous physical or mental suffering on
ALOOF	Distant physically or emotionally
AMBIGUOUS	Open to more than one interpretation
APPURTENANCE	Something added to another, more important thing; an appendage
BASE	The lowest or bottom part

BESEECH	To address an earnest or urgent request to
CARNAL	Of or relating to the body or flesh; bodily
CHURLISH	Difficult to work with
COMMINGLED	Mixed together
CONJURATION	Influence or effect by a supernatural power
CONTAGION	A harmful, corrupting influence

CONTRIVE	To plan with cleverness or ingenuity; scheme
CONVOCATION	Assembly
DISCORD	Tension or strife
DISCRETION	Ability or power to decide responsibly
DIVULGING	Becoming known
ENTREAT	To make an earnest request of

EPITAPH	An inscription on a tombstone in memory of the one buried there
EXTOLMENT	High praise
FELICITY	Great happiness; bliss
FILIAL	The relationship of child or offspring to parent
IMMINENT	About to occur; impending
INVULNERABLE	Immune to attack; impregnable; impossible to damage, injure, or wound

KNAVISH	Unprincipled
MALICIOUS	Spiteful
PARAGON	A model of excellence or perfection
PERDITION	Loss of the soul; eternal damnation
PERNICIOUS	Deadly; destructive; wicked
PITEOUS	Demanding or arousing pity

PORTENTOUS	Full of unspecifiable significance; exciting wonder and awe
PRODIGAL	Rashly or wastefully extravagant
REPLICATION	A reply to an answer; a rejoinder
SCOURGE	A means of inflicting severe suffering, vengeance or punishment
SINEWS	Tendon; muscles
SUPERFLUOUS	Being beyond what is required or sufficient

VISAGE	The face or facial expression
VOW	An earnest promise

Hamlet Vocabulary

COMMINGLED	EXTOLMENT	PERNICIOUS	REPLICATION	KNAVISH
PRODIGAL	BASE	DISCORD	DISCRETION	IMMINENT
SCOURGE	FELICITY	FREE SPACE	PORTENTOUS	VOW
ENTREAT	ALOOF	DIVULGING	VISAGE	CONJURATION
FILIAL	EPITAPH	CHURLISH	CONVOCATION	SUPERFLUOUS

Hamlet Vocabulary

SINEWS	AFFLICT	INVULNERABLE	CONTAGION	CONTRIVE
PERDITION	ABATEMENTS	AMBIGUOUS	APPURTENANCE	PITEOUS
BESEECH	PARAGON	FREE SPACE	SUPERFLUOUS	CONVOCATION
CHURLISH	EPITAPH	FILIAL	CONJURATION	VISAGE
DIVULGING	ALOOF	ENTREAT	VOW	PORTENTOUS

Hamlet Vocabulary

DIVULGING	INVULNERABLE	SUPERFLUOUS	DISCORD	BESEECH
CONVOCATION	IMMINENT	VISAGE	PORTENTOUS	CHURLISH
EXTOLMENT	EPITAPH	FREE SPACE	COMMINGLED	CARNAL
CONJURATION	BASE	SCOURGE	PERDITION	AFFLICT
PARAGON	PERNICIOUS	ALOOF	REPLICATION	ABATEMENTS

Hamlet Vocabulary

SINEWS	ENTREAT	VOW	PRODIGAL	CONTRIVE
MALICIOUS	DISCRETION	KNAVISH	AMBIGUOUS	APPURTENANCE
PITEOUS	FELICITY	FREE SPACE	ABATEMENTS	REPLICATION
ALOOF	PERNICIOUS	PARAGON	AFFLICT	PERDITION
SCOURGE	BASE	CONJURATION	CARNAL	COMMINGLED

Hamlet Vocabulary

CONVOCATION	DISCORD	CONJURATION	KNAVISH	PRODIGAL
BESEECH	SINEWS	INVULNERABLE	EPITAPH	SCOURGE
DIVULGING	PARAGON	FREE SPACE	SUPERFLUOUS	MALICIOUS
VOW	AFFLICT	EXTOLMENT	IMMINENT	CONTRIVE
PERDITION	APPURTENANCE	ENTREAT	PORTENTOUS	CARNAL

Hamlet Vocabulary

FELICITY	ABATEMENTS	CHURLISH	CONTAGION	AMBIGUOUS
DISCRETION	REPLICATION	ALOOF	FILIAL	VISAGE
PITEOUS	PERNICIOUS	FREE SPACE	CARNAL	PORTENTOUS
ENTREAT	APPURTENANCE	PERDITION	CONTRIVE	IMMINENT
EXTOLMENT	AFFLICT	VOW	MALICIOUS	SUPERFLUOUS

Hamlet Vocabulary

REPLICATION	AFFLICT	CONTAGION	BASE	IMMINENT
FELICITY	PERDITION	DISCRETION	INVULNERABLE	SINEWS
EXTOLMENT	DISCORD	FREE SPACE	ALOOF	PRODIGAL
MALICIOUS	AMBIGUOUS	APPURTENANCE	VOW	CONTRIVE
CONVOCATION	ENTREAT	PORTENTOUS	SUPERFLUOUS	COMMINGLED

Hamlet Vocabulary

CONJURATION	FILIAL	KNAVISH	CHURLISH	DIVULGING
CARNAL	ABATEMENTS	SCOURGE	PARAGON	VISAGE
PITEOUS	BESEECH	FREE SPACE	COMMINGLED	SUPERFLUOUS
PORTENTOUS	ENTREAT	CONVOCATION	CONTRIVE	VOW
APPURTENANCE	AMBIGUOUS	MALICIOUS	PRODIGAL	ALOOF

Hamlet Vocabulary

MALICIOUS	CONJURATION	CARNAL	DIVULGING	FILIAL
PITEOUS	CONVOCATION	ABATEMENTS	APPURTENANCE	PERDITION
REPLICATION	INVULNERABLE	FREE SPACE	BESEECH	EXTOLMENT
EPITAPH	ALOOF	SUPERFLUOUS	VOW	ENTREAT
PERNICIOUS	PARAGON	PORTENTOUS	DISCORD	AMBIGUOUS

Hamlet Vocabulary

FELICITY	IMMINENT	SCOURGE	VISAGE	SINEWS
CONTAGION	AFFLICT	KNAVISH	CONTRIVE	BASE
CHURLISH	COMMINGLED	FREE SPACE	AMBIGUOUS	DISCORD
PORTENTOUS	PARAGON	PERNICIOUS	ENTREAT	VOW
SUPERFLUOUS	ALOOF	EPITAPH	EXTOLMENT	BESEECH

Hamlet Vocabulary

COMMINGLED	PRODIGAL	ALOOF	INVULNERABLE	VISAGE
MALICIOUS	DISCRETION	DIVULGING	PITEOUS	CONJURATION
ABATEMENTS	EXTOLMENT	FREE SPACE	CONTAGION	ENTREAT
VOW	SCOURGE	KNAVISH	SUPERFLUOUS	BASE
EPITAPH	PERDITION	SINEWS	PERNICIOUS	DISCORD

Hamlet Vocabulary

FELICITY	CONVOCATION	REPLICATION	PARAGON	BESEECH
IMMINENT	AMBIGUOUS	CARNAL	APPURTENANCE	CONTRIVE
PORTENTOUS	CHURLISH	FREE SPACE	DISCORD	PERNICIOUS
SINEWS	PERDITION	EPITAPH	BASE	SUPERFLUOUS
KNAVISH	SCOURGE	VOW	ENTREAT	CONTAGION

Hamlet Vocabulary

ENTREAT	CARNAL	VISAGE	DISCRETION	SCOURGE
COMMINGLED	SUPERFLUOUS	PITEOUS	BASE	VOW
DIVULGING	FELICITY	FREE SPACE	APPURTENANCE	CHURLISH
PERNICIOUS	CONVOCATION	PRODIGAL	FILIAL	IMMINENT
BESEECH	AMBIGUOUS	CONTRIVE	MALICIOUS	CONJURATION

Hamlet Vocabulary

SINEWS	EXTOLMENT	PARAGON	PORTENTOUS	DISCORD
CONTAGION	AFFLICT	ALOOF	REPLICATION	ABATEMENTS
PERDITION	KNAVISH	FREE SPACE	CONJURATION	MALICIOUS
CONTRIVE	AMBIGUOUS	BESEECH	IMMINENT	FILIAL
PRODIGAL	CONVOCATION	PERNICIOUS	CHURLISH	APPURTENANCE

Hamlet Vocabulary

EXTOLMENT	CONJURATION	CONTRIVE	KNAVISH	ABATEMENTS
APPURTENANCE	INVULNERABLE	PERDITION	VOW	BASE
PARAGON	CONTAGION	FREE SPACE	PITEOUS	AMBIGUOUS
EPITAPH	CHURLISH	PORTENTOUS	DISCRETION	PERNICIOUS
DISCORD	DIVULGING	FELICITY	ENTREAT	FILIAL

Hamlet Vocabulary

MALICIOUS	COMMINGLED	VISAGE	PRODIGAL	SINEWS
ALOOF	BESEECH	AFFLICT	CONVOCATION	REPLICATION
CARNAL	IMMINENT	FREE SPACE	FILIAL	ENTREAT
FELICITY	DIVULGING	DISCORD	PERNICIOUS	DISCRETION
PORTENTOUS	CHURLISH	EPITAPH	AMBIGUOUS	PITEOUS

Hamlet Vocabulary

CONTAGION	AMBIGUOUS	PITEOUS	COMMINGLED	DISCORD
ABATEMENTS	ALOOF	VISAGE	EXTOLMENT	DIVULGING
SUPERFLUOUS	APPURTENANCE	FREE SPACE	FELICITY	INVULNERABLE
CONVOCATION	CHURLISH	SINEWS	PERNICIOUS	PRODIGAL
BASE	CARNAL	KNAVISH	MALICIOUS	AFFLICT

Hamlet Vocabulary

REPLICATION	IMMINENT	FILIAL	DISCRETION	PORTENTOUS
PERDITION	VOW	CONTRIVE	SCOURGE	ENTREAT
BESEECH	EPITAPH	FREE SPACE	AFFLICT	MALICIOUS
KNAVISH	CARNAL	BASE	PRODIGAL	PERNICIOUS
SINEWS	CHURLISH	CONVOCATION	INVULNERABLE	FELICITY

Hamlet Vocabulary

AFFLICT	CONJURATION	PORTENTOUS	CONVOCATION	EXTOLMENT
FILIAL	AMBIGUOUS	MALICIOUS	PRODIGAL	BASE
COMMINGLED	CHURLISH	FREE SPACE	VOW	PERDITION
DIVULGING	CONTRIVE	SCOURGE	VISAGE	DISCRETION
REPLICATION	APPURTENANCE	IMMINENT	CONTAGION	ALOOF

Hamlet Vocabulary

ENTREAT	PERNICIOUS	INVULNERABLE	FELICITY	DISCORD
EPITAPH	PARAGON	BESEECH	PITEOUS	SINEWS
ABATEMENTS	CARNAL	FREE SPACE	ALOOF	CONTAGION
IMMINENT	APPURTENANCE	REPLICATION	DISCRETION	VISAGE
SCOURGE	CONTRIVE	DIVULGING	PERDITION	VOW

Hamlet Vocabulary

VOW	SCOURGE	BASE	IMMINENT	COMMINGLED
APPURTENANCE	SINEWS	SUPERFLUOUS	FELICITY	EXTOLMENT
EPITAPH	AMBIGUOUS	FREE SPACE	DISCRETION	CONTAGION
CHURLISH	CARNAL	DIVULGING	DISCORD	MALICIOUS
PERNICIOUS	ABATEMENTS	FILIAL	CONJURATION	BESEECH

Hamlet Vocabulary

KNAVISH	INVULNERABLE	PITEOUS	REPLICATION	ENTREAT
AFFLICT	CONVOCATION	PORTENTOUS	PERDITION	PARAGON
ALOOF	CONTRIVE	FREE SPACE	BESEECH	CONJURATION
FILIAL	ABATEMENTS	PERNICIOUS	MALICIOUS	DISCORD
DIVULGING	CARNAL	CHURLISH	CONTAGION	DISCRETION

Hamlet Vocabulary

KNAVISH	CONJURATION	BESEECH	SUPERFLUOUS	CONTRIVE
PITEOUS	REPLICATION	SCOURGE	CONTAGION	AFFLICT
CHURLISH	COMMINGLED	FREE SPACE	CARNAL	VOW
CONVOCATION	SINEWS	EXTOLMENT	PERNICIOUS	INVULNERABLE
ABATEMENTS	MALICIOUS	FILIAL	ENTREAT	EPITAPH

Hamlet Vocabulary

AMBIGUOUS	IMMINENT	DISCORD	PORTENTOUS	FELICITY
APPURTENANCE	PERDITION	PARAGON	BASE	VISAGE
PRODIGAL	DIVULGING	FREE SPACE	EPITAPH	ENTREAT
FILIAL	MALICIOUS	ABATEMENTS	INVULNERABLE	PERNICIOUS
EXTOLMENT	SINEWS	CONVOCATION	VOW	CARNAL

Hamlet Vocabulary

AFFLICT	ALOOF	CONVOCATION	REPLICATION	ABATEMENTS
APPURTENANCE	EXTOLMENT	SCOURGE	DIVULGING	CONTAGION
CONTRIVE	FILIAL	FREE SPACE	CARNAL	SUPERFLUOUS
FELICITY	VOW	PERNICIOUS	MALICIOUS	PERDITION
KNAVISH	BASE	DISCRETION	SINEWS	EPITAPH

Hamlet Vocabulary

INVULNERABLE	VISAGE	DISCORD	PRODIGAL	CHURLISH
IMMINENT	AMBIGUOUS	PORTENTOUS	PARAGON	CONJURATION
COMMINGLED	BESEECH	FREE SPACE	EPITAPH	SINEWS
DISCRETION	BASE	KNAVISH	PERDITION	MALICIOUS
PERNICIOUS	VOW	FELICITY	SUPERFLUOUS	CARNAL

Hamlet Vocabulary

PRODIGAL	ALOOF	DISCRETION	REPLICATION	BESEECH
SCOURGE	SINEWS	DISCORD	FELICITY	MALICIOUS
EXTOLMENT	PITEOUS	FREE SPACE	CONVOCATION	PERDITION
SUPERFLUOUS	CARNAL	CONTRIVE	FILIAL	CHURLISH
AFFLICT	PERNICIOUS	COMMINGLED	ABATEMENTS	PARAGON

Hamlet Vocabulary

VISAGE	AMBIGUOUS	EPITAPH	CONTAGION	DIVULGING
BASE	PORTENTOUS	INVULNERABLE	CONJURATION	IMMINENT
APPURTENANCE	ENTREAT	FREE SPACE	PARAGON	ABATEMENTS
COMMINGLED	PERNICIOUS	AFFLICT	CHURLISH	FILIAL
CONTRIVE	CARNAL	SUPERFLUOUS	PERDITION	CONVOCATION

Hamlet Vocabulary

CHURLISH	FILIAL	PARAGON	INVULNERABLE	ABATEMENTS
CONJURATION	DIVULGING	PRODIGAL	ENTREAT	PITEOUS
CARNAL	DISCRETION	FREE SPACE	EXTOLMENT	AFFLICT
CONTAGION	EPITAPH	FELICITY	PERDITION	VISAGE
ALOOF	DISCORD	KNAVISH	PERNICIOUS	SUPERFLUOUS

Hamlet Vocabulary

PORTENTOUS	SINEWS	BESEECH	BASE	AMBIGUOUS
SCOURGE	APPURTENANCE	IMMINENT	CONVOCATION	MALICIOUS
VOW	CONTRIVE	FREE SPACE	SUPERFLUOUS	PERNICIOUS
KNAVISH	DISCORD	ALOOF	VISAGE	PERDITION
FELICITY	EPITAPH	CONTAGION	AFFLICT	EXTOLMENT

Hamlet Vocabulary

PORTENTOUS	ABATEMENTS	ALOOF	KNAVISH	EXTOLMENT
VISAGE	DISCORD	SINEWS	FELICITY	CONTRIVE
REPLICATION	PERNICIOUS	FREE SPACE	SUPERFLUOUS	PARAGON
SCOURGE	CONJURATION	ENTREAT	MALICIOUS	PITEOUS
BASE	APPURTENANCE	BESEECH	PERDITION	COMMINGLED

Hamlet Vocabulary

DIVULGING	EPITAPH	CONTAGION	AMBIGUOUS	PRODIGAL
CHURLISH	CONVOCATION	IMMINENT	VOW	DISCRETION
INVULNERABLE	CARNAL	FREE SPACE	COMMINGLED	PERDITION
BESEECH	APPURTENANCE	BASE	PITEOUS	MALICIOUS
ENTREAT	CONJURATION	SCOURGE	PARAGON	SUPERFLUOUS